PROMISES *of* REDEMPTION

The Failure and Triumph of a Wife, Mother, and Geneticist

JIN-CHEN CAMILLA WANG, MD

Interior Image Credit: Robert A. Dennis

ISBN: 978-1-6847-1055-3 (sc)
ISBN: 978-1-6847-1056-0 (e)

Library of Congress Control Number: 2019919984

Lulu Publishing Services rev. date: 01/09/2020

PROMISES
of
REDEMPTION

The Failure and Triumph
of a Wife, Mother, and Geneticist

A Memoir

JIN-CHEN CAMILLA WANG, MD

CHAPTER 1

UNTIL THE STORM PASSES BY

I was born in war-ridden China in late 1945, two months after Japan's surrender to the Allied forces, which effectively ended World War II.

Japan is a small multi-island nation located east of China with a total land area of only approximately 146,000 square miles, which is slightly smaller than the state of California. Other than fishing, Japan had virtually no natural resources. China, on the other hand, had been endowed with bounteous land—more than twenty-five times that of Japan—and endless treasure.

In 1937, imperialistic Japan decided to invade China for its vast assets of natural resources, such as minerals, coal, crude oil, natural gas, and iron ore since Japan lacked these resources. Human toll is unavoidable in any war, but the extent of the unspeakable monstrosities and war crimes that Japanese soldiers inflicted upon Chinese women and children were beyond comprehension for any reasonable human being. A Japanese newspaper recorded an incident that involved two Japanese soldiers wagering an unimaginably barbaric killing contest to see who could, with a sword, kill one hundred Chinese people first. This cruel incident was followed and documented by Japanese newspapers, a testament that the basic human decency could be lost amidst war and mob mentality.

No accurate numbers regarding the rampant mass torture, rape, and murder were obtainable; the estimates in the city of Nanjing alone during a six-to-eight-week period in late 1937 varied from forty thousand to more than three hundred thousand. The period was heartbreakingly described as the "Rape of Nanjing." Events surrounding the incident were carefully chronicled by writer and historian Iris Chang, who sadly took her own life at age thirty-six.

The numbers of civilian fatalities resulting from the unhinged brutality of Japanese soldiers would have been even higher if not for the efforts made by American physicians and missionaries working in Nanjing at the time. They established a Nanjing safety zone and sheltered many Chinese women from the inhumane and savage behavior of the Japanese soldiers.

One of the physicians in the group was Robert O. Wilson (October 5, 1904–November 16, 1967), the son of an American missionary. He was born in Nanjing and educated at Princeton University and Harvard Medical School. He returned to China in 1936. In a letter Dr. Wilson wrote to his family from Nanjing on December 18, 1937, he said, "Today mark sixth day of the modern Dante's Inferno, written in huge letters with blood and rape. Murder by the wholesale and rape by the thousands. There seems to be no stop to the ferocity, lust, and sadism of the brutes." He later testified as a Nanjing Massacre eyewitness at the International Military Tribunal for the Far East, exposing the unfathomable atrocities the Japanese soldiers brutally committed upon the Chinese people. According to one of Dr. Wilson's diary entries:

> Last night the house of one of the Chinese staff members of the university was broken into and two of the women, his relatives, were raped. Two girls, about 16, were raped to death in one of the refugee camps. In the University Middle School where there are 8,000 people, the Japanese came in ten times last night, over the wall, stole food and clothing, and raped until they were satisfied.

In memory of Dr. Wilson's heroic actions taken to protect ordinary Chinese citizens from the brutality of Japanese soldiers, a group of Chinese Americans organized a memorial service dedicated to him on November 12, 2017, eighty years after the incident of Rape of Nanjing—a much-delayed tribute to a man who was willing to stand up to the unconscionable Japanese soldiers and protect the voiceless Chinese citizens.

The memorial was held in the United Methodist Church in Acadia, California, where Dr. Wilson's father had once served as a minister. It was attended by an unexpectedly large crowd wishing to pay tribute to a selfless American who, along with a number of his colleagues, had remained in Nanjing to protect those left behind from the unspeakable crime of the Japanese soldiers during one of the darkest periods in China's history. Many of Dr. Wilson's relatives were also in attendance at the memorial.

After the service, a special plaque was erected in his honor in the church's courtyard. People stood shoulder to shoulder to witness the long-overdue recognition and acknowledgement rightfully owed to a righteous man. It was a fittingly humble place for a selflessly humble hero.

Like Hitler's Holocaust and concentration camps, the Nanjing Massacre was one of the most barbaric and disgraceful acts in the history of humanity.

* * * * *

The war between China and Japan lasted eight years, from 1937 to 1945, the last four of which became part of World War II when Japan launched a surprise attack on Pearl Harbor on December 7, 1941. As such, the United States was forced to react and enter into war. Prior to direct conflict between the United States and Japan, the public's general opinion had been mixed, and the polls had shown that the majority of American citizens opposed going to war against Japan.

The one-sided, unprovoked military action taken by the Japanese against the Americans woke up the people, and the country united behind its leaders to support the war against the Empire of Japan in response to President Franklin D. Roosevelt's call to "remember Pearl Harbor." It was a grave miscalculation by the Japanese government. By ignoring rules of engagement and stealthily bombing Pearl Harbor, Japan brought upon itself a fierce response from the US.

Four years later on August 15, 1945, Japan was finally brought to its knees and surrendered unconditionally to the Allied forces after atomic bombs were dropped on Japan's cities of Hiroshima and Nagasaki. The human toll of the war was high, especially for the Chinese, with an estimated total death of fifteen to twenty million. The toll for the Japanese aggressor was also high, around 2.5 to 3 million of its seventy-three million total population, while the United States lost around 410,000 lives.

After World War II ended in 1945, the ten-year civil war that had begun in 1927 resumed between the two major political parties of China: the Kuomintang Party (also known as the Nationalist Party), established in 1912, and the Communist Party, established in 1921. The civil war had been suspended in 1937 in order to form a united front to fight against the two parties' common enemy: imperialistic Japan. Ultimately the Kuomintang Party, to which my parents belonged, lost to the Communist Party in late 1949. The Kuomintang government retreated from mainland China to Taiwan, a small island approximately fourteen thousand square miles in size located 110 miles southeast of the mainland. Fearing for their lives, a mass exodus of people not belonging to the Communist Party ensued, my family among them.

Although direct communication between the two entities— People's Republic of China, established in 1949 and commonly referred to as China, and the Republic of China, established in 1912 and currently occupying the small island of Taiwan—was reestablished in the 1980s, they remain politically separate to this day.

* * * * *

Both sides of my family had been among the most prominent in their hometown for generations. They were renowned not only for their wealth but, more importantly, for having many scholars. They were widely known as "the family scented with the fragrance of books." Their love and respect for reading, writing, and knowledge could be traced back many generations. Inscribed on my great-great-great grandfather's tombstone were these words:

> To be respected, one must first be compassionate
> To leave a footprint, one must first be well-read
> Forever carry forward

The tombstone with its inscriptions was erected in 1891, one hundred and some years ago. In contrast, engravings on other tombstones mostly included phrases praising the dead. During a generation in China when illiteracy was more or less a norm, it was truly rare to be able to recognize the importance of being able to read and write. It was no accident that our family was among the best known and most respected in its township.

My maternal grandfather was a learned scholar, passing the imperial examinations in the early 1900s. My maternal grandmother passed away from complications of asthma when my mother was only fifteen. My grandfather was forty-six at the time; he never remarried, despite multiple entreaties from friends and unrelenting visits from matchmakers. He dedicated his life to educating the young; he set up classrooms and taught history, literature, and mathematics. My mother was among his students, and she described to us how my grandfather drilled into his students the importance and value of reasoning and understanding rather than memorizing and reciting. Not only was he an educator but my grandfather was also a fully engaged member of the society. He was among the first in his community to advocate for equal rights for women, a rather revolutionary idea in Chinese society at the time, which was met with skepticism initially. But he sowed seeds, even though it took many more years before women became an accepted equal class in Chinese society. When the civil war between the Kuomintang Party and the Communist Party ended in the withdrawal of the Kuomintang government to Taiwan, my grandfather refused to retreat with us; instead, he remained to fight an all-but-lost underground battle against the Communists in order to "succeed or sacrifice for my country." For the country he deeply loved, he was arrested, jailed, and finally lost his life at the hands of the Communists in January 1951. Communism, as a political party, forever became my mother's nemesis.

My paternal grandfather was also a respected scholar; he founded and taught in schools. He died of an unidentified illness in March 1945, seven months before I was born. He also vehemently promoted education for all—men and women—and was the first in his hometown to speak against the millennium-old peculiar and cruel practice of female foot-binding. For reasons perplexing to the rest of the world, small feet, or more accurately tiny feet, were perceived as a symbol of beauty in China beginning around the eleventh until the early twentieth century. It was said the practice was inspired by a tenth-century court dancer who bound her feet into the shape of a new moon, danced in it for the emperor, and received his favor. It became a widespread custom in China for many centuries and was considered a status symbol; women from wealthy families would not need their feet to walk for the purpose of performing chores and could therefore afford to have tiny feet. The practice involved tightly wrapping each of a young girl's feet with long strips of cloth beginning at four or five years of age. The toes were deliberately broken, and the cloth was pulled tightly to restrict foot growth. They would be unbounded regularly to clean and remove any debris and dead tissue and then were rebound even tighter. The feet were thus made artificially small in the shape of a lotus and were consequently known as "lotus feet."

I had seen my grandmother's bound feet when I was growing up. Every once in a while, after dinner, she would unwrap her long bindings and soak her deformed feet in warm water, slowly and methodically massaging them with a countenance of relief and contentment. She represented the last generation of women, in our family and among our neighbors at least, who had been subjected to this hellishly inhumane custom. My grandmother was otherwise quite healthy; other than a peptic ulcer that flared up intermittently, she enjoyed a long and active life. She died at the age of ninety-two from complications of pneumonia when I was in my fifth year of medical school. Unlike the American system where students were generally admitted to medical school only after they had already completed four years of college, medical school in Taiwan accepted high school graduates directly into the seven-year medical education program.

The Chinese used an expression to humor those who were chatty and unduly wordy: "Like the wrapping cloth old women use to bind feet: they are long-winded, and they stink."

* * * * *

Both my parents were from small families. My father had only one sibling, an older brother. My mother had one older brother and one older sister. When my aunt was dating the man who was to become my uncle, my mother would tag along with her sister to visit my uncle's home. My mother ended up spending much time with my uncle's only brother. Thus, my mother and my father were brought together fortuitously. Romances were cultivated that eventually resulted in a match of "two sisters for two brothers." It also meant we and our cousins are "double first cousins," sharing one-quarter of our genes instead of the usual one-eighth as is the case for most first cousins.

Our family had been living in Chongqing where my father worked for Kuomintang's air force, concentrating on military intelligence. He also took upon the responsibilities as a Morse code specialist. When the civil war intensified in 1949, he sent his family—my mother, my older sister, my infant brother, and me—back to join my grandmother in our then yet unscathed hometown of XiangShan, in the province of Zhejiang on the eastern shore. The two cities, Chongqing and XiangShan, were approximately one thousand miles apart.

The civil war raged on, and it was not too long before it became clear that Kuomintang was at the losing end. XiangShan was to face its unwelcomed yet unavoidable fate. In July 1949, a group of nearly two hundred Communist soldiers marched into our beautiful, serene, and resource-rich seaport town. My family probably had the largest house in the neighborhood, and the group came in and overtook our home, which had been designed and built by my grandparents. The buildings were constructed in the then popular style of Chinese quadrangle, a structure comprised of four interconnected buildings arranged in the shape of near-rectangle. In the center of the four buildings, a large yard was filled with plants, flowers, a goldfish pond, and a well that supplied one of the most essential elements of life: water. The soldiers forced us to move into the servants' quarters. I was not quite four at the time, and I was not sure if it was my own memory or if it was because of my mother's repeated painful recounts in later years; regardless, in my mind's eye I saw myself napping by the window, only to be awakened by the noises of the large group of soldiers in uniform. That image was deeply and permanently seared in my mind.

The Communist soldiers conducted political classes daily and performed regular military exercises and drills in and around our property. They were rather polite and well-behaved in the beginning. Once, they accidentally broke an ordinary glass jar and insisted on paying for it. Before long, though, they began to loosen their restraint, became less disciplined, and started to make various demands. They wanted to butcher a pig that my family had been raising. My grandmother would not agree to it as the pig was not yet fully grown, but she had to give in after the soldiers' continual pestering.

The soldiers also chopped down trees, cut the trunks and branches into pieces, and used them as fuel for cooking. When the wood chips were exhausted, they would chop down more trees. Stoves were on nearly all day long to feed the influx of large numbers of soldiers. The pristine fruit orchard on the west end of the property became littered, destroyed, and filled with a putrid odor.

Not long after, persecution of people in the township suspected of having connections with the Kuomintang Party began. As an educated and landowning family with ties to the Kuomintang, my family was an obvious target. However, being one of the most respected and beloved families in town, we were not overtly harassed. We were closely watched nonetheless. Like all other ordinary citizens, our lives were forever changed.

* * * * *

The war disrupted much of the country's communications system, and we soon lost contact with my father. Not knowing whether he was safe, my mother struggled to hide her anxiety and tried to provide assurance to my grandmother. From how quickly the Communists had been advancing, my mother already foresaw the ominous fate of her homeland.

My uncle—my father's only brother—held a high position in the Kuomintang government and was accorded the responsibility of taking charge of the eastern portion of the province of Zhejiang. He had wanted my grandmother and our entire family to move with his family to Putou, the township where his new job assignment was located, but my mother had lost contact with my father at the time and was afraid of not being able to reconnect if we moved away. My grandmother, reluctant to leave my baby brother, decided to stay behind with us and to provide company for my mother. The two women, mother and daughter-in-law, leaned on each other as they waited for dawn to mercifully descend. My mother was prepared to take action as soon as she received word from my father.

Months later, a letter from him finally came and informed us he had retreated with the government to Taiwan, the only safe place still under Kuomintang control. He had been working on obtaining the necessary documents for us to join him. Fearing interception by the Communists, the letter had passed through a number of trusted hands before reaching us.

My mother immediately began the process of preparing to escape under the watchful eyes of the Communist soldiers who now controlled our home—and our fate. She put the plan that had been incubating inside her for months into action. She made frequent short outings to accustom our captors to her comings and goings. She also took advantage of those outings to visit her friends and distant relatives, urging them to consider getting out. Most people, though, were afraid of the danger and trouble associated with fleeing and chose instead to remain in the comfort of the short-lived status quo. Their fateful decisions to stay proved, unfortunately, to have brought onto themselves many years of hellish life under Communist control in the Chinese mainland.

Because of the prolonged war and unrest the country had been continually experiencing, my paternal grandfather's coffin had not been buried. It had been kept on the west side of the property on the high grounds surrounded by fruit trees. My grandmother had been waiting for the arrival of a peaceful and auspicious time to be able to undergo the formal process of choosing the "right site" according to the "signs of wind and water" to bury my grandfather. Now, facing the reality of having to abandon her home, my mother had to make sure the coffin would stay safe and would not be robbed and destroyed amid the Communist occupation. With my grandmother's permission, she had a tomb built for it before embarking on our perilous journey.

Nearly four decades later, citizens of the two sides of the Taiwan Strait were finally allowed to visit one another. By this time, my grandmother had long passed away. My parents had her coffin exhumed and her remains collected and brought from Taiwan back to our hometown of XiangShan in the Chinese mainland. They also recovered my grandfather's remains, which had been kept safely in the tomb built just before we fled China. My grandparents' remains were finally kept together. During my first and only visit to my early childhood home in 2017, I was able to see their urns sitting side by side in a vertical cemetery tower in my original hometown.

As part of her escape plan, my mother tried to sneak some valuables out of the house prior to our journey. She had one of her menservants take a large basket of rice to my grandfather's house; she told her Communist captors it was part of her usual practice of charity to feed the less fortunate in the neighborhood. That practice had indeed been one of my mother's regular charities, but this time, it was part of her strategy in preparation for our escape. She had planned to use the rice to pay for our journey. The soldiers were suspicious, and they searched the basket to find an expensive clock my mother had wrapped with old newspaper and hidden in the bottom of the basket. Most of the soldiers had limited education and many were illiterate; they were not able to understand fully what was written on the newspaper, and they suspected it contained sensitive information or anti-Communist messages and propaganda. Instead of questioning my mother's intention, they put their suspicion on the newspaper and accused my mother of being a spy for the Kuomintang. My mother was suspended from leaving the compound.

My mother had been fully aware of the danger we were facing and had adjusted her outlook and expectations for life. She was psychologically prepared for the possibility of losing her life at the hands of the Communists. Her concern was the safety of my grandmother and her three young children. Fully aware she was the only one who could provide protection for us, she suppressed her own fear and continued her preparation for our escape.

When the period of her detention ended, she sent my grandmother, my little brother, my brother's wet nurse, and me to her father's home, using the excuse that my grandmother needed to visit and pay homage to Buddha for a few days and that the rest of us went along to keep her company. Only she and my older sister Ling, who had started first grade, stayed behind.

That night, my mother summoned the two servant girls who had been with our family for many years and said, "I already spoke with your parents. Tomorrow you are free to go back to your own homes. I am going to take Ling to my father's house to reunite with my mother-in-law. From there, we will try to flee to Taiwan. You have been with my family for a long time—now it's coming to an end. I only wish we would meet again."

The two girls burst out crying.

My mother, filled with mixed emotion of fear, anger, sadness, and sorrow, was unable to hold back her own emotions. She cried for the first time since her home was overtaken by the soldiers. In later years, my mother would think of those girls and wonder what had become of them. Sadly, she never saw or heard from them again.

The next day, my mother walked out of her home for the last time. To avoid arousing suspicions under the watchful eyes of the soldiers, she took nothing but a small purse she always carried on her outings. She told her captives she was going to the cemetery to pay respect at her ancestors' graves. She had already arranged with a distant cousin to take my sister out of school and to meet her at the foothills of the mountainous road that led to her father's house. She had been on this road many times before; it was the only way to her father's. Usually she sat in a sedan chair carried by laborers, but that day, she walked—and she crawled when the road became increasingly rough and rugged.

My mother left behind all material possessions, fully aware the journey we faced would be treacherous and the chance to come back and reclaim our home was practically nonexistent.

* * * * *

Our hometown, XiangShan, was a coastal town in southeast China. Our best escape route was by the sea to ZhouShan Island, the largest among the thirteen hundred islands of the ZhouShan archipelago just off the mainland to the east. ZhouShan was also where my uncle and aunt's home was located. We could stay with them before getting a ride to Taiwan on a military plane.

In the meantime, my mother continued her attempts to persuade her father to leave XiangShan and escape with us first to ZhouShan Island and then to Taiwan, even though she was fully aware that getting him to agree would be "harder than climbing Mount Everest." My grandfather insisted upon staying behind to assist the underground anti-Communist activities.

We stayed at my grandfather's house for a few days until the angry sea calmed down to a level reasonable for passing. My mother hired two small boats, bid a heartbreaking goodbye to her father, and in the darkness of the night, began the most dangerous segment of our journey out of our ancestral home.

The skipper wanted to distribute the weight evenly between the two boats, noting it could only be achieved by separating us into two boats.

My mother insisted that we all stay in one boat and let the second boat carry our belongings and the rice that was to be the payment for our journey. "We live or die together," she declared.

The skipper relented at last.

We had to pass seven Communist-guarded ports before we would be safely on the open sea. "Be absolutely silent when the boat is near the ports," the skipper warned. "Make sure adults don't cough and children don't cry."

We held our breath. My little brother who was usually described as "the crybaby" forgot to cry and remained silent.

It was after midnight when we safely passed all seven ports and were on the open sea. The sea was rough, and the waves were high. My brother's wet nurse vomited first, followed by my sister, me, my grandmother, and finally my mother. Only my baby brother was untouched by the stormy sea.

We reached our destination, ZhouShan Island, just as the sun was beginning to rise. A new day had dawned for my mother, and a glimpse of hope was finally in sight after her long and unrelenting nightmares. We stepped off the boat and walked toward my anxiously waiting uncle. To my grandmother and my mother, it was as if a lifetime had passed since they lost their home to the occupying Communists.

We stayed in my uncle's house until arrangements to enter Taiwan were completed. My mother realized the danger the country was in, and she knew it would be a long exile on the island of Taiwan for those who sought shelter from Communist brutality. She was right, unfortunately. But even she was not able to anticipate the lengthy time it took—more than thirty years—before people on the two sides of the Taiwan Strait were allowed to resume communication.

My mother had one more hurdle to overcome. My uncle was against letting my grandmother go with us. He worried she could not tolerate the one-hour flight on a military plane, and he believed ZhouShan, still under the Kuomintang control at the time, would stay safe.

The night before we were to leave our homeland and flee to Taiwan, my mother was tossing and turning in bed and trying to figure out a way to convince my uncle to let his mother go with us. She was finally granted a eureka moment. She suddenly realized she had been barking up the wrong tree. She was searching for a way to convince her brother-in-law; instead, she should have her mother-in-law convince him herself. She got up, went to her mother-in-law's bedside, woke her, and said, "Ma, I am taking the children and leaving for Taiwan tomorrow. Elder Brother wants you to stay. It is not that I worry they could not take care of you, but it is too chaotic here now. With your ulcer, it would be much better for your health if you come with us. If you decide to go, Elder Brother will not stop you."

My grandmother got up early next morning and began packing.

"Ma, you really want to go?" my uncle asked.

"Let me go, son. You all get ready and come join us soon." My grandmother understood the danger and misery that were to come upon ordinary citizens under Communist control.

At three-thirty in the afternoon of January 31, 1950, we stepped out of the military plane and rushed into the bosom of my anxiously waiting father.

In the chaos of two million people trying to flee from the mainland all at once, numerous families were broken apart. We knew of many such instances among our friends and neighbors, including my uncle's family.

* * * * *

Everyone in my immediate family escaped from the Communists, but my uncle's family was not as fortunate. My uncle, who had always believed ZhouShan would stay safe, finally faced the reality and decided to take his family and flee. Their two oldest daughters were in nursing school at the time and had already retreated with their school to Taiwan.

On that fateful day, the rest of their family—my uncle, aunt, and the remaining four of their six children—boarded a large boat in the morning destined for Taiwan. For unknown reasons, the boat stayed on the shore for a prolonged period of time. Since there was no sign it was going to start its voyage anytime soon, my uncle and aunt decided to get off and go home to retrieve some additional belongings of theirs, leaving behind their four young children with the maid who had been the youngest boy's wet nurse. When their parents did not return after quite some time—and fearing the boat might take off—the maid sent the oldest boy to go back to fetch them. In the meantime, the boat began its voyage.

In the chaos of the mass exodus, no one paid attention to the three young children. The oldest of the three, seven-year-old Pearl, threw herself on the deck and cried herself to sleep. She was forced to grow up hastily; she woke up and became the maternal figure to her younger sister and brother.

Not knowing what to do, they got off the boat when it stopped at a small island. There were some military personnel and families living in the buildings on top of the hills. The maid found an abandoned small temple at the foothills and made it their temporary home. They lived on wild plants, dead fish that had been washed ashore, and whatever else they could find. Gradually people began to leave, and the population on the island dwindled. With no real means to survive, the maid decided to take the three children and return to their hometown.

While some families welcomed an extra hand to help with daily chores, no family could afford to support three extra mouths all at once. Those families that decided to remain in their homes either lacked means to allow them to complete the escape process or naïvely believed life under the Communists would not be much different from what they had been used to.

Pearl and her two siblings were forced to be separated into different households. They were also shuffled around, and at times, they had to beg for food. The maid, whom the youngest boy referred to as "Mama," remained in contact with them and did her best to care for them.

Life was utterly miserable, but Pearl managed to keep in touch with her siblings all the while. One winter, while walking across an empty field, she saw her brother digging for wild plants, a basket by his side. Choking, she asked why he was all alone. "Ma told me to pick plants for dinner," he answered, calling the lady of the house where he was staying "Ma." The sky was gray; snow was going to fall. Pearl took her brother's freezing hands; in tears, she helped him gather some more wild plants before hurrying him back to his temporary shelter. In her many sleepless nights in the days and years that followed, she was to be haunted by that image of her brother's tiny figure, carrying a basket too big for his body, walking away from her in the bitter cold.

Pearl did everything she could to care for her siblings. Life bestowed no mercy on the three young children—or on the majority of ordinary citizens under the Communist sovereignty. Poverty was rampant, and the three youngsters had to be bounced around from home to home with no prospects for a real or long-term arrangement.

Four long years later, in 1954, when Pearl was ten, a distant relative brought a message that their mother and older brother were in Shanghai and were searching for them. Her mother, my aunt, who was from the most respected family in our hometown and who never before had to work for food, had taken upon the menial work of a seamstress.

Ever since they were separated from their parents, Pearl had felt as if she had been in a prolonged, never-ending nightmare. Deep in her heart, she had dreamed of the day when she would wake up to find her parents there for her. *Did the day finally come? Is this the day I finally wake up?*

In Communist China at the time, moving residence was not a personal choice; permissions from the local government were required, and the process could be quite lengthy. Pearl immediately began the task of obtaining all the necessary approvals and documentations to move their registrations from XiangShan to Shanghai, a distance of approximately 170 miles. Her mother had asked her to move first to help with the sewing business.

Pearl had been dreaming of reuniting with her parents for years. She wanted to be by her mother's side instantly, but what would happen to her younger siblings if she left first? She convinced her mother that her little brother should go first, then her sister, and only then herself. She walked an entire day for a round-trip distance of approximately thirty-five miles on the rugged land with hills and valleys, not stopping for lunch, to complete the application processes. She did this three times over a span of nearly two years for her siblings and finally for herself.

The family that was broken apart and left in the mainland when the Communists overtook the country was finally reunited in Shanghai. Unfortunately, as if all the miseries the family was forced to endure were not enough to redeem themselves from the anger of a furious God, disasters continued to strike the family without mercy. To add to the already monumental tragedies, Pearl's younger sister was killed in a bicycle accident years later after the family finally settled down in Shanghai.

* * * * *

My uncle, who had been confident that his home in ZhouShan would stay safe, at last realized he was in a most precarious state. Because of his high position in the Kuomintang government, he was considered an archenemy of the Communists and was vigorously sought after. Communist soldiers had been to their home multiple times in search of him. For him, it was literally "flee or die."

By that time, a mass exodus of the population not belonging to the Communist Party had already been set in motion. Like most people, my uncle's destination was Taiwan, the small island off the southeast coast of mainland China, which was a place safe for those with any connection with the Kuomintang Party.

My uncle and aunt left ZhouShan immediately and went to Shanghai to stay with a distant relative while making arrangements to flee to Taiwan. Shanghai, unlike ZhouShan, was a large city, and it was easier to hide from the Communists. There, they put their escape plan to action. My uncle was to travel south by himself; my aunt was to stay behind. They, unfortunately, did not anticipate any danger befalling my aunt since she had no political connections and would not be a target of the Communists.

Wary of raising suspicion by the train conductor of a man traveling south alone in the direction of Taiwan, my uncle and aunt bought a train ticket and a platform ticket to Guangzhou, the capital city of the province of Guangdong at the far southeast corner of the country, pretending my uncle, holding the platform ticket, was seeing my aunt off. It was less likely to arouse suspicion if a woman was traveling south in the direction of Taiwan than a man. Once the conductor had checked tickets, my aunt exchanged her ticket with my uncle and got off the train with the platform ticket. She went back to stay with a distant relative, apparently believing the chaos was only temporary. Indeed, she was not singled out for persecution, but she failed to foresee the drastically harsh life for the next forty years that was to come upon her and upon all ordinary citizens left in mainland China.

From Guangzhou, my uncle was able to get to the nearby Hong Kong and then onto Taiwan to join us. He was a devoted son and came to our house to visit my grandmother every Sunday without fail. With his wife and four of their six children left in the mainland and no communication between the two sides of the Taiwan Strait, his wounds were deep—and his regret was without bounds. He often resorted to drinking to numb himself. More than once, my father had to bail him out of jail for drunkenness and public nuisance.

It was not until more than forty years later that the borders were beginning to be opened on both sides of the Taiwan Strait. After the long and agonizing separation, my mother was finally able to travel to Hong Kong to meet with her sister who traveled from Shanghai for the long-awaited reunion. My uncle, who had become a heavy smoker and drinker, had been struggling with lung cancer for quite some time and was at the terminal stage of his illness.

While my aunt and my cousins in mainland China were anxiously waiting for arrangements to be made for the reunion to take place, my uncle succumbed to his illness. My parents had to hide the news of his passing from my aunt initially, using the excuse that my uncle was traveling out of the country on business and could not be reached. My uncle did not last long enough to reunite with his wife and his four children left behind in the mainland when the Communists overtook China. The day he and my aunt decided to go home to retrieve additional belongings and thus missed the boat sadly became the last time he would see those closest and dearest to him. And I finally understood why my uncle would risk his health with heavy smoking and perpetual alcohol abuse.

That was the tragedy of their generation.

* * * * *

Recently, my siblings and I took a trip to China to trace our roots. China had recently enjoyed rapid progress in leaps and bounds and was no longer the same China my family had fled from. Luxury and affluence were everywhere, but the land of our old homestead stood vacant. China had so much land and such abundant resources; it might be easily understood why vacant land was a common sight in rural areas. Still, I was rather disappointed to see only a large tree and an old dried well remaining on what had been our property. I had been expecting to see a large mansion in the style of a quadrangle, somewhat run-down perhaps, but grand and imposing nonetheless. It amazed me when I suddenly realized that sixty-eight years had passed since my mother took us and fled from our homeland of mainland China.

We met up with many of our relatives for the first time in our lives, most of whom I was not even aware I had. It was pouring rain when we landed in our hometown of XiangShan in the province of Zhejiang. We were immediately surrounded by the large group of relatives, close and distant, who had been waiting to welcome us.

For the next five days, we were treated as royalty, driven around to visit our many relatives, close and distant, and fed mouth-watering delicacies every day and every meal, including breakfast. Pearl, who was now in her early seventies, came with her younger brother—the one she tried desperately to protect during the early Communist days— from a neighboring province where they now resided. Pearl recalled vividly the day her parents missed the boat. She waited anxiously at the bow, straining her eyes every time someone approached, wishing they were her parents. She recounted her horrific life experiences growing up under Communist control. While she was able to let go the memories of many nightmarish events, she could never forget the image of standing as a representative of her family amid a group of adults, listening to lectures giving by their captors on how and why they should be grateful for their Communist "liberators." This she related to me in a choking voice. She was not quite eight at the time.

Pearl had always wondered what had detained her parents that day the family was to board the boat and began their journey together to Taiwan. She wanted to ask her mother, but she eventually decided it might be better left unasked and unanswered.

To this day, my oldest cousin who came to Taiwan with her nursing school staff still lamented her mother's failure and my mother's wisdom. "Aunt brought every one of her children safely to Taiwan—not a single one was left behind," she bemoaned repeatedly. Two sisters, two utterly different fates.

Besides my uncle's family, I knew of many in our neighborhood who had some members of their families trapped in mainland China. I was reminded of how blessed my siblings and I were to have had a mother who was fully wise and courageous.

* * * * *

As soon as he arrived in Taiwan, my father began looking for temporary housing for us. With the sudden influx of huge numbers of people, building shortages were a serious problem. As we were waiting for air force-provided accommodation to become available, my father found and rented a small one-room shack that he could afford. A shack indeed—the floor was all dirt; the walls were brick, straw, and mud. There, the entire family of seven, including my baby brother's wet nurse, crammed in.

My mother soon found a full-time desk job in the city's police department to help support the family. Later, she learned the art of embroidery and spent all her "free time" at night making decorative needlework and selling it to supplement our living expenses.

My uncle was a good artist, and he would sketch pictures for my mother to embroider over. My mother became exceedingly good at it; she was later encouraged by our neighbors and friends to enter competitions. At least two of her works won prizes. It came with a heavy price, though. The long periods of sitting and hunching over while she stitched put much strain on her body, and she suffered from a peptic ulcer with bouts of severe stomachaches ever since.

I was young and ignorant at the time, and I did not quite realize the sacrifice my mother made for us. My sister Ling described it in her journal: "Late at night, I lay in bed listening to the sound made by the needle passing through the tightly stretched fabric, one stitch after another, continually. It was as if my heart was being stabbed, repeatedly and unrelentingly." My eyes welled up every time that image of my mother, hunching over the cloth stitching, came into my consciousness. It hit me like a brick.

Peony, one of my mother's embroideries that won competition. My uncle, who was also a gifted artist, made the sketch. This work was included in the collection of the art museum in Taiwan. It was later damaged by water when a fire broke out at the museum. The water stain is evident, especially in the lower right corner.

Another one of my mother's embroideries that won a prize.

* * * * *

In front of our first home in Taiwan, the one-room shack, my sister and I played in a small, gentle stream where the local women washed their clothes. By that time, my little brother was no longer nursing, but my parents had kept his wet nurse since she had no relatives and no place to go.

One day, when my sister and I were playing by the river, the wet nurse brought our brother to us and left him in our care while she worked around the shack. My brother followed us around with a small plastic cup in hand to scoop water from the river. Unaware of the magnitude of the responsibility asked of us—we were six and four years old then—we paid little attention to him. My brother fell in the river.

Local Taiwanese women were washing clothes on the river banks, but no one made any attempt to rescue him. Since most people were poor in those days, it was not too unusual to see an abandoned infant in the waters.

I never knew how long my brother was in the water or how my father found out, but an image was permanently seared in my mind. I saw my father running along the river bank and then carrying my brother's body in his arms. Solemnly and without a word, he went to my mother's workplace to bring her home. He was too distraught to speak a word to her.

For days and weeks afterward, I would be awoken at night by sounds of sobbing. My mother would never get over the pain of losing my brother. Even in my adulthood, she would still talk to me about him and about her unquenchable agony. She had risked her all to keep her family whole when the Communists overtook our home in the mainland, only to lose one of her children to a devastating accident. How could one reconcile a tragedy so grave and so senseless?

But there was no blaming. The wet nurse remained in our home. Only after I became an adult did I realize the profound wisdom of my parents. Nothing could bring back my brother. Not anger, not reproach, not condemnation.

Years later, our wet nurse remarried. She kept contact with our family and remained loyal to my parents all her life.

* * * * *

Not too long after the drowning of my brother, our family was finally allocated a small two-room apartment unit in a housing complex built for air force personnel and their dependents. We moved away from that sad dwelling by the river.

Our new home was in a village that consisted of rows of ten two-room, single-story units linked together. There was no private toilet; toilets were shared and located in separate buildings scattered throughout the complex. There were no bathtubs or showers either; people used washbasins and recycled water for all washing and cleaning purposes. Both my parents were from highly privileged families, but like most people, they adjusted quickly and uncomplainingly.

My father, who was very resourceful, took advantage of the space at the back of our unit and built a makeshift shower. He also used bamboo plants as supporting poles to construct a lattice over the walkway in front of our apartment to grow vegetables and fruits. Harvests from my father's efforts were usually plentiful; the surplus was enough to feed many of our neighbors. Building codes were nonexistent at the time; the small island of Taiwan was only in the initial stage of being adapted to become homes for the multitude of people who fled the Communists in mainland China.

In the center of the complex, the children took over a large, unpaved, open space and used it as a playground. My sister, a friend next door, and I learned to ride a bicycle there. Late at night, when no other children were outdoors, the friend's father would put us on the bicycle, push it, and let go. We cried and yelled, but we learned to ride quickly.

The grounds also doubled as an outdoor theater, and old movies were sometimes played as the main source of entertainment for all the residents of the village. Life was tough, but there were lots of playmates of all age groups coming from all parts of China. We enjoyed our time growing up, unaware of the much better material life beyond the confines of this unassuming collection of homes.

My family stayed in that village until 1957 when I graduated from elementary school and was to begin junior high. The apartment was too small for a household of seven, including the wet nurse who later moved away after she was remarried. My father applied for a larger dwelling. After a long wait, we were finally allocated a unit with attached individual toilets in a newly constructed group of homes. Our new home was at the end of a row of six connected units. We enjoyed one of the largest yards among our neighbors, and it extended all the way to the border of the village, where a small stream demarcated the boundary. It was more than a step up for us.

* * * * *

My grandmother had regarded my little brother as the Wang family's "lifeblood" since only he could pass on our family's "Wang" name. My parents had no preference for a boy or a girl and had not planned for more children. With the passing of my little brother, they had to try for another boy, mainly on my grandmother's account. That brought me my beloved sister Grace, six years younger than I. Two years later, the only son in the family, my dear brother Shenandoah, arrived.

Shenandoah was naturally and undoubtedly my grandmother's favorite. Under her protection, he was able to play pranks on his three older sisters. He would gather small insects—butterflies, dragonflies, fireflies, and the like—let them free to roam inside the house, and laughingly watch his sisters screaming and yelling. He also enjoyed chasing after us and throwing small pebbles at us. Somehow, we never harbored any ill feelings against him; quite to the contrary, we endeared him. My parents loved and treated their four children equally and fairly, without any favoritism. I believe it was their wisdom that taught us to remain close to one another throughout our lives.

My sisters and I loved our grandmother even though she favored our brother. She was a great storyteller and had a special way of telling stories that captured our fascination. We especially liked stories of ghosts and fables. Huddled around her at night, scared yet anxiously anticipating, we were never tired of the one in which she described an ordinary-looking woman who removed her head nightly, put it on the table, and meticulously combed its hair.

My mother resigned from the city's police department and stayed home to keep my grandmother company. She had once serendipitously showed a neighborhood child how to solve a math problem. Word got out, and more and more children came to seek my mother's help. Some of our neighbors encouraged my mother to start a math tutorial service. Taking the advice, my father had two additional rooms built attached to our existing structure; the front room was my mother's "classroom," and the back room housed a bunk bed for Grace and me. I slept on the lower bunk, and Grace slept on the upper bunk.

My grandmother was happy to have my mother by her side all the time. When my mother taught and coached her students, my grandmother helped with washing and preparing food for cooking. Whenever my mother had a break from teaching, she would go to the kitchen to see my grandmother and ask if she needed anything.

My grandmother always told my mother to take a rest if she had a free moment, telling her there was no room for two people in the kitchen anyway. Many of our neighbors mistook them as mother and daughter rather than mother and daughter-in-law.

My father was also busy around the house whenever he was off from work in the evenings or on weekends. He planted many fruit trees and dug a fish pond to raise fish. He also had two additional freestanding units built on the far end of our large yard and rented them out to supplement our living expenses. Later, when my older sister was married, she and her husband moved into one of the units. My father spent as much time as he could with us and took us around visiting places: the zoo, the botanical garden, the airport to watch planes taking off and land, the train station to see trains coming in and leave, and occasionally to the movies. The Chinese-subtitled delightful musical *Seven Brides for Seven Brothers* was one of our favorites; it made an everlasting memory of our carefree childhood.

Although materially poor, it was a rich childhood filled with love and fond memories.

My grandmother lived a long and generally healthy life. She died of heart failure in 1967 at the age of ninety-two when I was in my fifth year of medical school (the medical school curriculum in Taiwan consisted of four years of classroom instruction, two years of clinical rotation, and one year of internship). The cemetery was up on the hills, and it was drizzling on the day of her funeral. My family walked behind the pallbearers in the procession. Approximately halfway up, a heavy weight suddenly came upon the pallbearers, and they were unable to move forward. They put down the casket.

The monks walking alongside pleaded, "Esteemed madam, have mercy on the family. Please accept this temporary resting place. They will move you back to be with your late husband as soon as we retake your homeland."

The pallbearers picked up the casket without any difficulty and carried it straight up to the burial ground. The promise that my grandparents' remains would be brought together was fulfilled nearly twenty years later when the two sides of the Taiwan Strait, mainland China and Taiwan, resumed communication in the latter half of the 1980s.

I stayed in that home until thirteen years later, in 1970, when I graduated from the medical school of National Taiwan University and came to the United States for further advanced studies. My country, the government of the Republic of China, had given me six years of elementary education, six years of junior high and senior high education, and seven years of highly coveted medical education—fully free of tuition and fees. All expenses associated with my education from elementary through medical school were covered by scholarships and financial aid. I reaped all the benefits of a high-quality educational system throughout my formative years.

Family photo, 1963, the year I began medical school. My mother is standing behind my grandmother, my older sister Ling is sitting by my father, and I am sitting on the grass between my brother, Shenandoah, and my sister Grace. Our banana tree is in the background.

CHAPTER 2

MY MEDICAL EDUCATION IN TAIWAN

Seven Years of Studying and Fun

Countless lives were drastically changed by the catastrophic destructions brought on by World War II, which was followed soon afterward not by peace but by the resumption of the civil war between the two major political parties of China: the Kuomintang Party and the Communist Party. The war between the two parties had begun in 1927 but was suspended in 1937 during World War II in order to form a "united front" to fight both parties' common enemy: Japan.

Japan eventually surrounded to the Allied forces after atomic bombs were dropped in Japan's cities Hiroshima and Nagasaki. But with the resumption of the civil war soon after WWII ended in 1945, peace remained elusive for the Chinese people. Eventually, the Communists succeeded in taking control of China. The Kuomintang party retreated to Taiwan; my family was among the mass that followed the Kuomintang in the exodus.

Like us, the vast majority of families that survived the mass exodus had lost most if not all their wealth and possessions in the process. As a result, other than elementary schools, which generally admitted students based on the geographic locations of the students' residencies, government-subsidized public schools in Taiwan at any level—junior high, senior high, and college—became the most coveted path for youth seeking higher education. Competition for admission to these schools was extremely fierce. Students resorted to private schools only if they failed academically to secure a place in a public school. Consequently, during my time, the quality of public schools in Taiwan was generally much higher than that of private schools.

I had been mercifully endowed with the gift of quick learning; I usually did not need to spend much time studying. My daily routine was comprised of going to school, working on my homework as soon as I returned home, "book satchel still on her shoulder," as my grandmother and my mother affectionately commented, going outdoors to play once homework was done, having dinner, going out to play again, and going to bed at eight o'clock or nine on Sundays.

A radio drama program was played regularly on Sunday evenings from eight to nine. It was one of the few free entertainments available to us, and I usually stayed up for it. Since my grades were always among the highest, my parents left me alone, never reminding me to study. This habit of finishing homework before doing anything else was apparently the complete opposite of my older sister. I was told by my mother and my grandmother in later years that she would leave her homework assignments untouched until Sunday nights—just before bedtime. While I could never understand the philosophy of "play first, study later," she was nonetheless also able to succeed in being admitted, by examination, to the same prestigious National Taiwan University with a major in history.

Like all elementary school graduates, I took the obligatory citywide junior high admissions exam and was accepted to the school of my first choice. To reward the few top performers, each senior high school and college set aside a small number of places for high performers and admitted them without them having to sit for admissions exams. I was fortunate to be one of them. So, with one exam required across the board to get in junior high, I sailed through six years of junior and senior high education. Then, when the most competitive field of medicine offered itself to me without my having to go through the examinations process to secure a place, I grabbed it and began my lifelong journey in medicine.

This privilege of being automatically accepted to the Department of Medicine of the National Taiwan University was granted to fewer than twenty or so students among tens of thousands of high school graduates across the entire island. Thus, I went into medicine not because I had dreamed of being a doctor or because I had a desire to save humankind but because the opportunity was presented to me on a silver platter.

My decision was further cemented when I overheard a conversation between my parents. My father said, "It would be nice to have a doctor in the family."

Therefore, in the summer after high school, while nearly everyone else was studying furiously trying to score well and be admitted to a good college, I and a few fortunate others enjoyed blissful relaxation knowing the door to college had already been opened for us.

* * * * *

Our class had seventy students; it was one of the largest among all the departments of the National Taiwan University. Only thirteen of the seventy were females. While still quite disproportionate, the gender gap had begun to close slowly by then.

The vast majority of my classmates were native Taiwanese. Unlike those of us transplanted from mainland China when the Communists overtook it, they had been in Taiwan for generations. During the fifty-year period from 1895 to 1945, Taiwan was ceded to Japan as a result of China losing to Japan in the First Sino-Japanese War (August 1, 1894–April 17, 1895) fought between China's Qing Empire and imperialistic Japan. Taiwan was finally returned to China after Japan surrendered to the Allied forces at the end of WWII in 1945.

During the long Japanese occupation, Taiwanese people were severely persecuted and looked down upon by the Japanese except for those in the medical profession. Partly for this reason, doctors were generally highly revered, and the medical profession was universally coveted by the Taiwanese. Thus, as soon as the results of the admissions exam were announced and publicized, homes of the few lucky men who were accepted to medical school would be flocked with matchmakers guaranteeing large dowries from families longing for a doctor son-in-law. I knew a number of such instances in my class, but most of my male classmates, nearly all Taiwanese, preferred finding partners on their own. A number of them succeeded in marrying our female classmates.

Since the common language of all my friends and peers during my growing years was Mandarin, the official language of the country, I had never learned the Taiwanese dialect. While the written language of Chinese was largely the same across the country, the spoken language was vastly different among people who came from different parts of the land. Generally, each province had its own specific dialect, and the differences could be so huge that people from different provinces might not be able to understand one another. For me, I could not comprehend most words spoken in Taiwanese. My new classmates in medical school were very considerate; they always changed their conversation from their much more comfortable Taiwanese to not-so-fluent Mandarin whenever they saw me approach. I fully appreciated their thoughtfulness, although, on the flip side, it hindered me from learning Taiwanese. To this day, I am still quite ignorant of the spoken Taiwanese language.

In the fall of 1963, I began my seven-year journey of medical school—and I never looked back.

* * * * *

My medical school in Taiwan was on a seven-year schedule, three years longer than the usual four-year college degree programs. The other majors that had more than four years of curriculum were dentistry (six years) and medical technology (five years).

While the medical school curriculum was by and large similar in Taiwan and the United States, the processes of admission to medical school were quite different. In the United States, generally only students who already had a college degree could be admitted to medical school—usually regardless of what had been their major in college. In Taiwan, all high school graduates were in the same pool. They took the same island-wide college admissions exam and were admitted according to their performances in the highly competitive written examinations. For those fortunate few who were accepted to medical school, the degree offered at the end of the seven years was a bachelor's degree—the same as college students of any other major. It was recognized as equivalent to an MD degree in the United States, but only after additional clinical training in this country had been obtained and medical license examinations had been successfully passed.

Although the discipline of medicine had been generally perceived as "extremely tough" and a misconception prevailed that all medical students were bookworms, most of my classmates found such sentiment an exaggeration. Our course load might be heavier than many other departments, but we did not think we were under constant or undue pressure; we studied hard, but we also played hard, just like college students of any other major.

The first two years of medical school was roughly equivalent to a premed major in the United States. All classes were conducted in the main campus of the National Taiwan University and included such general subjects as Chinese literature, English, calculus, chemistry, physics, zoology, botany, psychology, and sociology.

Beginning in the third year, our home base moved approximately two and half miles from the university's main campus to the medical school campus where all classes took place. Subjects that had been rather general in scope began to transform and be more focused and specific. The highlight among all was undoubtedly the laboratory portion of anatomy. With anxious anticipation, it rolled around when the third year commenced. I was quite fainthearted in general, not with blood—the sight of blood never bothered me—but with darkness, imaginative goblins, ghosts, and anything associated with death. Having to face autopsy had been my only concern, if any, in going into medicine in the first place. I had to prepare myself psychologically for performing autopsies and studying various parts of the human body. Fortunately, with all my classmates around, none of whom showed signs of hesitation, it was not long before I was able to shake off my fear—but I was never brave enough to be in the gross anatomy room alone. Additionally, the odor of formalin that was utilized to preserve corpses was unrelentingly unpleasant; it lingered even after I walked away from the room.

I did what I needed to do—participated in performing autopsy and studied and memorized the names, locations, and functions of organs and tissues—but I could not pretend anatomy was one of my favorites.

The final exam for the anatomy class was set up in the autopsy room with multiple stations, each having a specific body part marked and a question attached. I could not remember how I did on the exam, but my final grade for the class was eighty-eight on a scale of zero to one hundred. By this time, I had already readjusted my perception of grades. Unlike in high school where anything below ninety or even ninety-five was considered disappointing, now amidst a class of top-rated students on the entire island of Taiwan, eighty-eight was no longer a very disappointing score for me. All my classmates were the elites of their respective high schools; I could not, and had no intention to, hold onto the status of "the best" I had long enjoyed.

Clinical practice started in the fifth year in our medical school and lasted for two years. This was when direct contact with patients began. There were still classroom instructions, but part of our time was spent on clinical rotation in various departments as "clerks." The curriculum included all medical specialties: internal medicine, surgery, pediatrics, obstetrics and gynecology, ophthalmology, otorhinolaryngology (ENT: ear, nose, and throat), neurology and psychiatry, dermatology, public health, and laboratory diagnosis. These rotations exposed us to real-life patients and sometimes their heartbreaking journeys.

One patient made an everlasting impression on me during my rotation in the Internal Medicine Department. He was an elderly man with end-stage hepatoma, one of the most common types of liver cancer in Taiwan. He had no family and apparently no friends. He was severely jaundiced, and his abdomen was massively distended with ascites (abnormal accumulation of fluid in the abdomen), a frequently observed symptom and sign associated with cirrhosis of the liver. As I stood by his bedside taking history and gathering information for the progress notes I was required to write in his medical records, he took my hand and began sobbing. He died shortly after that encounter. I had to deal with the heavy emotional burden of grief that people in the field of medicine sometimes have to unfortunately and unknowingly carry.

The seventh and last year of medical school was a hands-on rotating internship. No longer were there any formal classroom instructions, but our load was amplified rather than diminished. As interns, we were involved in all aspects of patient care: admitting patients to the hospital wards; taking medical, social, and other relevant histories; performing physical examinations; drawing blood specimens for various laboratory tests; completing necessary initial workups including performing hands-on laboratory tests such as CBC (complete blood count) and urinalysis, which, by the way, were done by laboratory technicians in the United States rather than medical students or interns; writing admissions notes and follow-up progress notes; prescribing orders; and starting intravenous lines.

The intern, together with the resident assigned to the patient, was responsible for both the initial workup and all aspects of subsequent follow-up care until the patient was discharged from the hospital. Night calls, usually every third or fourth night, were part of our responsibility in addition to our regular work. On busy nights, we would have to jump right into the new day after having been up almost all night. Somehow, we were able to adapt and function rather adequately, although there were times when I felt my mind was all jumbled up and my legs were walking on clouds.

During this internship period, one of the chief residents in medicine began to show interest in me. On the nights when I was on call, he would assign me to the less busy wards—and he would come to linger around where I was working. When I was leaving Taiwan for America, he somehow found out my flight schedule and came to the airport to see me off. I greeted and acknowledged him politely, but then I went right back to my family to continue our conversation and bid our farewells. That was the last time I ever saw or heard of him.

Weekly Grand Round was part of the curriculum. It was a highly intellectual exercise attended by the professorial staff, residents, interns, and sometimes other paramedical personnel. Enigmatic, difficult, or unusual cases were presented and discussed. These exercises broadened our exposure and knowledge; they were one of the highlights of our curriculum. Thesis was optional, and most of my classmates did not care to bother with it.

I spent the summer before my seventh year working in the laboratory designing and performing experiments under the guidance of my thesis advisor, Dr. Huang. My topic was "The Effect of Stress on Protein Metabolism: Urinary hydroxyproline excretion after fever-induced stress in rats." The presumption was based on the observation that stress such as burn, cold, heat, and infection caused an increase in urinary nitrogen excretion, reflecting an altered protein metabolism. Using rats as experimental animals, I sought to define the mechanism behind this conclusion. I was able to complete the research and successfully demonstrate that stress caused an increase in the breaking down of a protein named collagen in the body, which was then excreted in urine. Word processing was not available to us in 1969 and 1970, and I had to type and retype my thesis multiple times, but I was rewarded with an "excellent" grade in the end.

Since night calls were part of the responsibilities of interns and residents, the hospital provided housing for us during our last year of medical school. The dorm buildings were located at the far end of a long hospital hallway. A few weeks before my graduation, my mother came to my dorm unexpectedly and brought me a beautiful necklace. I had never been a jewelry person, and I rarely wore it—even though I loved its design immensely. Decades later, when my house in California was broken into and my few valuable pieces of jewelry were taken, the one my mother gave me before my solo journey to this country was spared. For no particular reason, but as if with premonition, I had decided to wear it to work moments before I stepped out of the house that morning. When my mother handed it to me in my dorm, she said, "You have never made me worry, emotionally or financially." I had been awarded merit scholarships enough to cover tuition, fees, and expenses for all the years I was in school.

That necklace remains one of my most treasured possessions to this day.

My most treasured jewelry. A gift from my mother shortly before my medical school graduation.

* * * * *

Not long after the first year of medical school started, those of us who were "locals" began to invite the "out-of-towners" for home-cooked meals after school and on weekends. We were young then, and it was easy to make friends at seventeen or eighteen. For my female classmates, one popular and favored activity was making dumplings together from scratch. My mother and my grandmother would help me prepare the dough and dumpling wrappers and fillings, and my new friends from school and I would put meat and vegetable fillings on the wrappers and seal them by pressing the sides of the wrappers together. Friendship and camaraderie were built quickly as we shared food and time together. As far as I know, we were a cohesive class: healthy competition, never backstabbing.

Our class also continued to observe the tradition of semiannual class outings to various popular tourist attractions around the island— at least during the first few years of medical school as far as I can remember. These were school-sanctioned activities where students were allowed to be absent from class as a group for a one- or two-day trip to a popular tourist attraction chosen and voted on by all members of the class. Those excursions were always highly anticipated and anxiously awaited moments.

One year, our destination was one of the most visited mountains in Taiwan, the Alishan (Mount Ali) in central Taiwan. It encompassed a mountain range of approximately 160 square miles. With many overlapping peaks, the view was at once stunning and inspiring. We hiked high up and stayed in a rather primitive accommodation for the night. It was so cold I suffered frostbite—as did a number of my classmates—but we were young and were not deterred.

Getting up before dawn, we waited for the sun to rise. Before us was a sea of clouds. Waves and waves of what looked like soft cotton stretched beyond what our eyes could see. It was enticing; it made one want to jump into nature and its wonder. In time, a sliver of light appeared that was followed by the grand entrance of the day. And, after an initial reluctance, the sun quickly leaped out to announce its unfailing presence and indomitable mightiness. It was worth the frostbite that kept my toes purple for a number of days afterward.

These outings were always welcomed breaks for us. A number of my classmates were good singers, and they would lead the class in singing such popular songs as "Jasmine Flower," "In That Distant Place," and "Small Town Story" as we happily and innocently wandered about on mountain roads, enjoying nature, appreciating scenery, smelling sunshine, and relishing our time together.

The music and the lyrics of "Jasmine Flower" along with memories of our leisurely strolls appeared in my mind's eye:

Beautiful jasmine flower
Beautiful jasmine flower
Fragrant and fully bloom.
White and pure without flaw
Let me pluck you with care.
For my love and my sweetheart
Jasmine, oh, Jasmine.

… … … … … … … … … …

Such were the happily memorable moments, the images of which floated into my consciousness every now and then in later years. It unfailingly sank me into nostalgia.

Studying for the GRE (Graduate Record Examinations), National Taiwan University campus, 1970. The exam was a prerequisite for application to American graduate schools. After graduation, all three of us received scholarships for additional advanced studies: Jane (left) at University of Illinois, I (center) at Purdue, Teresa (right) at Cornell.

* * * * *

With few exceptions, our class did well academically, and the vast majority graduated on time. A few of our classmates found the medical curriculum too rigorous and decided to transfer out of the department, thus abandoning their dreams for careers in medicine. Most of my classmates remained in Taiwan after graduation and went on to private practice in their respective hometowns. Many of them, though, eventually came to the States to continue their medical practices. All had been quite successful when judged by the size of their practices. Some of us chose academia or research and attained professorial-level status in reputed universities and hospitals. Our school educated and prepared us well, and almost all became contributing members of society either in our hometowns or our adopted country. Sadly, we lost two of our classmates to illnesses before graduation, a merciless reminder that mortality was universal—and no one could be immune even at a young age.

After seven years of what some people might consider a gruesome journey, I decided not to go into practicing clinical medicine, which had been the path of the vast majority of my classmates. The love for research and laboratory work always lingered over my heart and unrelentingly drew me back to it. Besides, I was never a people person, and I knew I lacked the people skills necessary for success in a purely clinical setting. Instead, I followed my calling and turned to laboratory medicine. It proved to be a wise choice and a most rewarding experience for me. I was one of the few in my class who did not remain in clinical practice.

Nevertheless, I was fully recompensed for having an MD degree under my belt. It afforded me with expanded credentials that included both basic science and clinical medicine. The convergence of which prepared me for a career in medical genetics, a field that encompassed practical medicine and basic research, and that was to become my most cherished career path.

Family photo, 1970, a few months before my medical school graduation. My older sister was not in this picture.

CHAPTER 3

STUDENT LIFE IN THE UNITED STATES

Just as I Am—Without One Plea

My love for research prompted me to strive to expand my credentials and seek additional postgraduate education in science. My thesis advisor in medical school, Dr. Huang, had spent a one-year sabbatical at the Massachusetts Institute of Technology (MIT) in Boston. He encouraged me to seek further education and secure an additional degree in the United States. Following his advice, I began applying for graduate schools in the semester prior to graduating from medical school. My ambition was to work for an additional PhD degree before starting a career in medicine.

I was accepted to a few graduate programs. Without hesitation, I decided on Purdue University since it was one of the most popular colleges for students from Taiwan at the time. Within two months of my graduation, I said goodbye to my parents, siblings, friends, and the place that had nurtured me all through my growing years. With a one-way ticket, I arrived in the States near the end of August 1970. Perhaps it was the excitement of going abroad, or perhaps it was because "a newborn calf fears no tiger," but I was not terribly sad or distressed for going so far away, alone. My mother, though, had many sleepless and agonizing nights for many months to come. In one of my older sister's letters, she wrote that my mother frequently "woke on her pillow stained with tears" during the early days of my departure. It was only later when I experienced those unshakably heart-wrenching worries about my own sons that I was able to fully understand the sacrifices parents willingly and unconditionally endured for their children, no matter how old they were.

There were a number of students on the plane going overseas like me. One of them, Luke, was also an MD from the same National Taiwan University and had graduated a year ahead of me. The policy in Taiwan at the time required all male college graduates to complete a mandatory one-year military training before being allowed to leave the country for advanced studies. It was at a time when the political relations between the two sides of the Taiwan Strait—the mainland China and the small island of Taiwan off the coast of southeast China—were nebulous at best, and tension existed with both sides claiming to be the only legitimate representation of China. The policy of a mandatory military training of all college-age men was possibly put in place in the event of war breaking out between mainland China and Taiwan. An urgent need to recruit soldiers who had at least some training was necessary under such circumstances. Fortunately, that fear never materialized. Now, more than forty-five years later, the two sides have resumed communication, and citizens across the Taiwan Strait are now free to visit one another.

Luke's sister and brother-in-law lived in the San Francisco area. Luke invited me to spend some time with his family and take the opportunity to sightsee and tour the city as my first introduction to the country. At the time, San Francisco was the most widely known American city among citizens in Taiwan. With my parents' permission, I accepted the invitation.

My final destination was West Lafayette, Indiana, where Purdue was located. I was going to study under the guidance of Professor Edward Simon in the Department of Biological Sciences at Purdue.

My first impressions of the country that was later to become my own were the vastness, quietness, cleanness, and a welcoming environment free of rude sounds of blasting horns that were unfortunately a constant street scene back home. Public transportation was the norm in Taiwan; very few families owned private vehicles in the sixties and early seventies. I had been used to seeing buses, taxies, and sometimes privately owned vehicles weaving in and out of traffic in chaos and hearing the annoying sounds of blasting horns almost constantly as if to announce their drivers' misplaced sense of superiority. Now, with the stunning view of the famed Golden Gate Bridge in the background, the streets of San Francisco were almost too quiet for me. The only sound I could hear was that of wind as cars swooped by. Never once did I hear the noise of a roaring car horn.

Everything in the States was new to me, including the minutiae of the way beds were made. It was quite different from how we did it back home; we usually just folded up everything and stacked them together. Bedspreads, which I had never seen before in my homeland, felt like a luxury to me. But it was visually pleasing, and I soon learned to use it after I had my own bed in my dormitory. When Luke's brother-in-law pulled into a gas station, it was the first time I saw how gas tanks were filled. I remembered seeing the price of gas being around twenty or thirty cents per gallon. I reflexively calculated in my head how much it was in Taiwanese currency, but it did not mean much to me anyway. We did not have a car, and I never paid any attention to gas stations back home—let alone gas prices. I was amazed, though, to realize the current gas price in San Francisco was more than ten times that in 1970 when I first arrived in this country.

I enjoyed the view of the sloped streets; the deep blue sea; the amazing sunset over the Pacific Ocean; the majestic nearly nine-thousand-foot-long (1.7 miles) Golden Gate Bridge between San Francisco and Marin County, one of the wealthiest American cities; and, of course, China Town, which was characteristically littered and noisy, unlike many other areas of San Francisco I had been introduced to.

We also visited the impressive Stanford University campus where Luke's brother-in-law had served as a faculty member. Stanford was a private and highly competitive university located near San Francisco.

Covering close to thirteen square miles (approximately eight thousand acres) of land, its campus is one of the largest in the United States. To the eyes of a newly arrived visitor, I considered it both majestic and imposing. Nevertheless, I was prejudiced and believed the main campus of the National Taiwan University was as beautiful and magnificent as Stanford. Only land was scarce, and buildings were much more intimately situated in my alma mater in Taiwan.

* * * * *

After an eye-opening experience and a very enjoyable introduction to this country, I was ready for my new home in my new land. Three days later, I flew to my final destination: West Lafayette, Indiana. My prospective advisor, Professor Edward Simon, had arranged for one of his colleagues' graduate students to assist me with my transition to this foreign land half a world away from my hometown. Nathan, also a National Taiwan University graduate, had been corresponding with me at Dr. Simon's request to prepare me for the rather drastic change in my life. A graduate student of Dr. Simon's colleague, Nathan had just completed his second year in the same Department of Biological Sciences where I was to begin my studies. He came to Purdue two years before me and was expected to graduate with a PhD degree within two additional years.

When Nathan picked me up at the airport, my immediate impression was about the length of his hair. It was not quite as long as a girl's hair—but at a length rarely seen on men back home. During my student years before college, girls were required to keep their hair short, straight, and not to let it grow beyond the tips of their earlobes. Boys almost always had their hair trimmed close to the scalp. These hair codes were strictly enforced before college: "You come to school to learn and not to show off with your hairstyle," we were told. Those requirements were relaxed once we became college students, but a long-haired male student was nonetheless a rare sight in Taiwan. It was a new sight for me, and I murmured to myself, "Such long hair!"

Nathan drove me to my first home in the United States and settled me down in a large multistory dormitory building designated for graduate students where I had preregistered with his help before my arrival. Most dorms in this high-rise had double rooms furnished with two single beds, two desks with chairs, two cabinets, and shelves attached to the wall. They were simple but adequate for a graduate student away from home. It was still a week or so before school was scheduled to start. The dorm was quiet with only a few of us coming from overseas. My assigned roommate, a West Virginia native, had not yet arrived. I unpacked my luggage after Nathan left. Pushing the empty suitcase to store it under my bed, an emotion of loneliness and sadness suddenly engulfed me. I went to bed teary and homesick.

The next day, Nathan took me shopping. It was not that I needed anything—just a first exposure to American life. Prior to leaving Taiwan, my entire family had spent days meticulously helping me pack for the long overseas trip. With a huge suitcase, I brought everything we could think of—down to buttons, needles, and thread—to make sure I had whatever I needed to start a new life in this faraway land.

We came to a building with this sign in front, "J. C. Penney Co." Brand-new to this country, I had no idea what those words meant until we went inside, and I realized it was the name of a department store full of all kinds of merchandises. Everything I brought from my homeland I could find in this store.

While JCPenney never became a favorite of mine, it would remain a nostalgic store in my heart, along with the small on-campus ice cream parlor Nathan often took me in the deep of winter during my first year at Purdue. I was never able to shake off those images of sitting in his heated red Camaro, watching snowflakes fall, eating ice cream, and listening to classical music on his car radio. It was heavenly, and somehow that wintry image invoked an everlasting nostalgia and stubbornly refused to leave my consciousness. Once, with the radio on, we left the car run idling for too long, and its battery died. It was an unknown experience for me, and I panicked. In the snow, Nathan walked me back to my dorm. He then returned with a friend to where he had left the car and jump-started it.

Purdue University, 1970. Taken the second day of my arrival.

* * * * *

My transition from a completely sheltered and confined life on the small island of Taiwan to a place half a world away was unexpectedly smooth. Sure, I missed my parents and siblings; I constantly thirsted for letters from home, and I wrote to them nearly every day in the beginning. Checking my mailbox became the first priority after returning to my dorm building from classes. I was able to assimilate rather quickly into the culture that had been entirely unknown to me prior to leaving Taiwan.

One major difference between students in the United States and students in Taiwan of my time was the way classroom instructions were delivered and received. In Taiwan, we had long been taught that teachers were guardians of absolute truth, and their words and commands were accepted by us students automatically without any question. Instructions were usually one-directional; students listened and spoke only when specifically asked to. No one ever challenged anything coming from their teachers' mouths. It took me quite some time to get used to the active participation in American classrooms—and sometimes even disagreements between students and their professors. Students here were not afraid to ask questions and express their own views. After witnessing a number of these interactions, I began to realize that teachers were not infallible; they too had limitations and could at times make mistakes.

Dr. Simon was one of the most popular and favored professors in the Department of Biological Sciences at Purdue during my time as a student in 1970–1971. Tall and lanky, he was always upbeat, kind, affable, energetic, and had a great sense of humor. His classes were very popular, highly energized, and well-received. His pop quizzes, though, could be hard and sometimes tricky. He welcomed me with genuine affection and warmth. Instead of a workspace in a corner of the laboratory like most other graduate students were provided with, he had a small office cleared out for me.

To introduce me to one of the great American pastimes, he organized a barbecue cookout for his entire laboratory staff, including all of his graduate students and laboratory technicians in the early days of my arrival. That's when I made my first blunder in communication. Dr. Simon had asked one of his PhD students to pick me up and drive me to the picnic grounds. Since I was new to the country and did not yet have a good understanding of the colloquial language, I misinterpreted the appointed pickup time of "ten of eleven" as "ten minutes after eleven" rather than "ten minutes before eleven." My ride had to call me after waiting in his car for too long while I was still sitting in my dorm patiently waiting for 11:10 to arrive.

Under Dr. Simon's guidance and following his suggestions, I took five classes with a total of nine academic credits in the first semester, which was considered a full course load. My classes included the three-unit Genetic Biology, a very popular but not very easy subject taught by Dr. Simon. It was my first true introduction to genetics, which was later to become my most cherished field of concentration. My other classes were General Biochemistry, Nucleic Acids, Seminar in Interferon, and Independent Research PhD Thesis.

I studied hard, and I played hard on weekends: movies, picnics, apple picking, and carnivals. For those outings, there was no trouble getting rides from male students who owned automobiles. In fact, most such opportunities were voluntarily offered to us girls. They would come to our dorm, pick us up, and drive us to wherever we needed to go.

I also had my first exposure to the Jewish religion by witnessing Dr. Simon practicing Judaism with such customs as wearing a kippah (a brimless cap) and eating only kosher foods prepared in specific ways according to the regulations of Jewish dietary law. Dr. Simon also observed the Sabbath, which was a day of rest from work beginning Friday evening just before sunset until Saturday night after three stars had appeared in the sky. In Jewish culture, it was a day in remembrance of God's creation of the heavens and the earth: "Thus the heavens and the earth were finished, and God rested on the seventh day from all the work that he had done in creation."

With an academic record of straight A for the semester, I enjoyed a very rewarding first experience as a graduate student in this then foreign country. I repeated this strong performance during my second semester at Purdue.

* * * * *

After my first year at Purdue ended and during the summer break in 1971, I moved from the university-owned graduate student housing to one of the many private apartments around campus. That was how most graduate students structured their living arrangements. They stayed in the dormitory during the first year and then moved to off-campus facilities that were usually less expensive and generally provided more freedom. Three other girls and I, all National Taiwan University graduates, rented a large remodeled three-bedroom basement with its own private entrance. Our landlord was an older American lady who owned a number of properties around campus. The rent was reasonable, and our landlord was friendly. She also responded to our needs readily. We settled in easily and comfortably.

I stayed there for seven months until the day I left Purdue at the end of 1971.

Our apartment became one of the favored gathering places around campus, especially for male students. On weekends, they would drop in on us, and we would all sit or lie on our carpeted floor and talk and exchange our thoughts and ideas. We enjoyed chitchatting, gossiping, and serious topics—our outlooks on life, politics, and almost everything else.

My three roommates and I shopped for food together every Friday evening and paid all the expenses from our common fund that we each contributed to equally. We took turns cooking and had dinner together every night. Although I had never cooked by myself prior to leaving Taiwan, I was able to learn rather quickly and fulfill my end of the duties reasonably well.

So many years have passed since our Purdue days together, and we have long drifted apart—we all had our own dreams and our own fates to follow. Nevertheless, those student days remain an endearing slice of life in my memory.

* * * * *

Shortly after my first year at Purdue ended and summer break began, a letter from Luke came inviting me on a trip to Niagara Falls. He was doing postgraduate studies at the University of Michigan, also on a research assistantship. Michigan was located north of Indiana, and the two schools, Purdue and Michigan, were approximately 270 miles apart. Luke and I had exchanged a few letters since I visited and stayed at his sister's home in San Francisco when I first arrived in the States. In those letters, we mostly described to each other our coursework and experiences in the new land. At the time I received his invitation, I was sort of on the rebound from a treasured yet short-lived relationship at Purdue. To give myself a chance to stay away from the sadness I had been experiencing, I accepted the invitation and took a Greyhound bus north to Michigan to meet up with him.

Niagara Falls was located near the international border of the United States and Canada. The falls were as grand and breathtaking as was popularly portrayed in movies, books, and photographs. With as much as six million cubic feet of water going over the falls every minute, the sight and sound of this natural wonder were altogether beyond intoxicating and exhilarating.

But the trip ended our friendship. Discussing dreams for the future during the long Greyhound ride, Luke indicated he "merely" wanted to be a practicing physician in a small rural community that could be expected to bestow a comfortable life of no pressure but pure enjoyment.

And I, too naïve to accept the reality and too inexperienced to understand the true meanings of success, was full of misplaced confidence and pride. I refused to be satisfied with a future filled with "only" daily routines of seeing and treating patients. To my yet untested mind, I considered it devoid of the drive to achieve the ultimate goal of existence: reach for the moon and stars and search for greater things and breakthroughs in medicine. I was too young, too self-reliant, and too proud; my hopes were too high, too ambitious, and too impractical. Regardless, it became clear to me that his goal in life was vastly different from mine, and the divide between us was too deep to mend.

Many years later, I realized I never did achieve that ultimate goal I envisioned for myself: to reach and hold the moon and the stars. However, I am at peace with what I did achieve, and I never once regretted parting with Luke.

* * * * *

The Niagara trip did not heal the sufferings I imposed on myself from that ill-fated and short- lived relationship at Purdue. While coursework continued to go well, and I maintained my strong academic performance, the excruciating toll of not being able to hold onto the one I truly treasured was beyond what I could bear. It put me in a state of virtually constant gloom.

Prior to leaving Taiwan for the United States, I had been fully prepared mentally to work for a PhD degree before beginning a career in medicine. Now coming back to Purdue from Niagara, my fragile emotions continued to unrelentingly eat at my soul. I was not able to let go of that self-imposed depression I dug myself into. I was so emotionally distraught that, a few months into my second year, while working on my experiment in the laboratory, I dropped an expensive cuvette as I was trying to put it into the spectrophotometer. It broke, and the small amount of radioactive content spilled onto the floor.

An overwhelming feeling of terror mixed with inextinguishable sadness over the failure of my relationship encompassed me instantly. I let loose my long-repressed emotional despair and began sobbing. The image that followed seared deeply into my memory.

Professor Simon squatted down next to me and helped me clean up. With consoling words, he reassured and comforted me. I broke down and admitted my emotional distress and requested to end my pursuit of a PhD degree.

As a father figure, Professor Simon gently advised me not to make rash decisions. However, I remained gloomy and was not able to resurrect myself from my deep depression. He eventually accepted my request. Not wanting to see me leave without having achieved my ambition in academia and since my performance had been rather extraordinary, he made a recommendation to the Biology Department to award me an MS (Master of Science) degree. I had only been at Purdue a year and four months by then. At the time, a master's degree would typically take at least two years of study. He also wrote glorious recommendations for me to pursue a career in clinical medicine. That was the first and only detour I ever made in my long years of pursuing a medical career. My original plan was to obtain a PhD degree before starting a career in medicine.

Years later, when I was working as a medical and laboratory director in California, Professor Simon visited me during a trip to the West Coast. I took him around and toured our laboratory in Pasadena. He showed much interest in what I had been working on in the field of genetics and was apparently happy to see what

I had achieved. That was the last time I saw him. He passed away in October 2006, after forty-six years of service to Purdue's Department of Biological Sciences. He will always be a gentle giant in my heart. And Purdue, even though I had to desert it under such sorrowful circumstances, will forever hold a special place in my soul.

CHAPTER 4

CLINICAL MEDICINE
IN AMERICA

The Point Is to Understand

I left Purdue for clinical medicine at the end of 1971 after having spent a year and four months in the place that had been my first home in this faraway land. I applied and was accepted to a one-year joint internship program in medicine and pediatrics at the Greater Baltimore Medical Center in Baltimore, Maryland. The internship combined trainings in both pediatrics and internal medicine and started at the beginning of January 1972, perfect timing for me since I had just finished up my journey at Purdue. Most internships and residency programs began in July; it was rare to find a position that accepted interns at the beginning of the calendar year.

With heavily mixed emotions, I packed up my life at Purdue, arrived in Baltimore, and reported to the hospital. As I was looking through the postings on the hospital bulletin board, I found a "room for rent" note. I took down the address and visited the American family who placed the note. Their home was a very attractive two-story craftsman-style house. There was a covered front porch with pillars lining the entry that was three or four steps above the ground. The house had a sloped roofline, overhanging eaves, a fireplace, and a large yard. Commuting to work was easy; it was only a short walk to the bus stop, and from there, a few miles on a bus to the hospital. Without hesitation, I excitedly rented a room from them and settled in. The family soon invited me to join them for meals whenever I was not on call and was home from the hospital. Since I had never been interested in cooking—my cooking experience at Purdue was purely out of necessity to fulfill my share of responsibility—and I had never really learned the art of cooking, I enthusiastically requested to change our arrangement from simply renting a room to room and board.

My landlords and I grew close quickly, and in no time, they became my "adoptive" parents. I became a member of their family. My adoptive mother's widowed sister also lived with them. Every night after dinner, the two sisters would do the dishes while I sat in the kitchen watching them and chatting with them continually. They told me what was happening in the neighborhood, and I told them about the successes and failures I encountered with patients we treated at the hospital. We grew so close that when I was married and had my own children, my sons became their "adoptive grandchildren."

My adoptive mother never tired of retelling the story of how fascinated my sons were with the exquisite cuckoo clock sitting on top of their beautifully carved redwood buffet table. Every time we took the children to visit, the boys would stand in front of the clock, watching intently and waiting for the singing bird to stick its head out to cuckoo and chime. The family remains dearly in my heart to this day, many long years after they all passed. They had a musician daughter a few years younger than me, and we reconnected after my first novel, *The Triumphant Life,* was published more than forty years after we met.

During the year I was in Baltimore, a PhD student in his last year of pursuing his doctoral degree in aerospace science at Purdue visited me every two or three weeks. I had met him in the early days of my arrival at Purdue, and he had been fiercely after me ever since. The driving distance between Purdue and Baltimore was nearly 650 miles. Driving straight in good weather, the journey took more than ten hours each way; it took much longer in the winter. Once on a snowy day, he was involved in an accident on his way back to Purdue. He was not seriously injured, but the car suffered extensive damage and had to be towed. In my rather bewildered and disconcerted state, I married him before the end of the year. My landlords took him in as their adoptive son-in-law.

*   *   *   *   *

The internship at the Greater Baltimore Medical Center was my first experience in clinical medicine in this country. From then on, my career concentration fluctuated between clinical and research, depending on my husband's career direction, which dictated where we lived and what opportunities were available to me. This path might have been a blessing in disguise as it exposed me to both the clinical arena and the research arena. It provided me with expanded credentials along with a tremendous advantage over my career options later on.

Although interrupted intermittently by both my husband's and my own career moves, I was eventually able to complete the three-year clinical training (one year internship at Greater Baltimore Medical Center and two years residency at North Shore University Hospital in Long Island, New York) required to qualify for medical license examination, which I took as soon as I fulfilled the requirements and passed without much difficulty. To me, those three years of clinical training and experience also affirmed the importance of knowledge. One example stood out when I was in Baltimore for my first year of clinical training in this country.

A six-year-old boy was admitted to the hospital due to a sudden onset of severe jaundice and abdominal pain. Jaundice is the medical term describing a yellowing of the skin and the sclera. Sclera is the opaque layer of the eye known colloquially as the "white of the eye." Besides jaundice, the only abnormal physical finding was a slightly enlarged spleen. The parents were from a Mediterranean country, and they remarked that the child had rather severe and prolonged jaundice requiring phototherapy while he was a newborn.

I spoke with the parents, took the patient's medical history, performed a physical examination, wrote admission notes, and presented the case to the attending physician and my fellow interns during our regular morning bedside rounds. The attending asked the parents, "Did he have any fava beans recently?" With an affirmative answer, the diagnosis of G6PD (glucose-6-phosphate dehydrogenase) enzyme deficiency was made and later confirmed by laboratory tests.

This enzyme deficiency caused red blood cells to break down prematurely, a process known as hemolysis, which can lead to anemia and jaundice. G6PD deficiency is most commonly observed in people of Mediterranean or African origin. Factors that triggered the process of hemolysis in patients who were deficient in the G6PD enzyme included intake of certain foods, especially fava beans, viral or bacterial infections, and certain medications.

G6PD deficiency is a genetic disorder inherited in an X-linked recessive pattern. X-linked inheritance describes a mode of inheritance when the gene in question resides on the X chromosome. Recessive indicates a person will have manifestations of a genetic disease only when both copies of the gene, one on each of the same pair of chromosomes, have the same defect. A female who has a mutation of the G6PD gene on one of her two X chromosomes would be a carrier of the disease but would not be affected clinically since she also has a normal copy of the gene on her other X chromosome. A male, on the other hand, has only one X chromosome. He would therefore show manifestations of the disease if his only X chromosome, which he inherited from his mother, carries the mutation. Ingestion of fava beans by these individuals could increase the level of some oxygen-containing chemicals in their blood, causing red blood cells to be destroyed faster than the body can replace them, resulting in anemia and severe jaundice.

The boy was treated with intravenous fluids and soon recovered. Since his hemolysis was not severe, a blood transfusion was not required, and only a conservative approach of treatment with fluid and close monitoring were needed. The parents were advised that the child should always avoid ingesting fava beans.

This case made a tremendous impression on me; it taught me the power of knowledge. Because the attending physician was able to make the diagnosis quickly, the child and his family were spared any unnecessary physical and emotional anguish.

* * * * *

I completed my one-year internship at the end of 1972, and my husband obtained his PhD degree at around the same time. He was offered a postdoctoral research position in aerospace science at Cornell University in Ithaca, New York. Ithaca was a small college town in south-central New York. Considered one of the most beautiful college campuses in the country with gorges and waterfalls all around, Cornell was also among the forerunners academically. We moved to Ithaca in the beginning of 1973, settling down in an eight-unit, two-level apartment complex on a large gentle slope. It was surrounded with grass and roses. During the fall, the entire region was set ablaze with the colors of nature. It was a dizzying and dazzling view of nature at its best.

I made a cold visit to Cornell's Department of Biochemistry, Molecular and Cell Biology, and I introduced myself and asked if they had a research position for someone with an MD degree who was interested in research. I was referred to one of the principal investigators in the department and took an on-the-spot, hands-on test to determine the molecular weight of an unknown chemical substance. I did well and was immediately accepted as a postdoctoral research associate in the department. Interestingly, the salary of a postdoctoral member in universities was generally lower than that of a bachelor-degreed technician whose job usually involved performing whatever tasks were dictated to them. Fortunately, obtaining experience and credentials was more important to me than financial compensation.

I liked my work in research, but a part of me wanted to fully capitalize on my seven years of medical education and be recognized and licensed to practice medicine in this country—even though clinical practice was not my ultimate goal in my pursuit of a career in science and medicine. To be eligible for license examination, obtaining formal clinical training in this country was a prerequisite. I began to explore training opportunities. After a short search, I was invited to join a two-year residency training program in pediatrics beginning July 1, 1974, at the North Shore University Hospital/Cornell University Medical Center in Long Island, New York, 260 miles from Ithaca. My husband encouraged me to seize the opportunity; he was willing to take the more than four-hour drive from Cornell to visit me and our one-year-old son whenever he could. It was a good opportunity, and I took it. I sought my parents' help. My mother had visited and helped us when our son was born, and this time, my father came from Taiwan to take care of our son while I worked. We rented an apartment in a high-rise building on the hospital grounds. The apartment faced the pediatrics wards, and I could see our apartment from the nurses' station. It soon became a habit of mine to glance at the window blinds of my apartment to see if my son was napping. When he was old enough to sit well by himself, my father would put him on the back of his bicycle and take him out while I worked. One afternoon, a surprise rainstorm suddenly started without warning. I immediately left work, got in my car, and drove around to look for them. My father stayed with us until I completed the two-year training in June 1976. It was a long two years for him to be away from my mother and his friends back home, but he enjoyed the time spent with us.

In the meantime, my husband completed his postdoctoral training at Cornell and was offered a position in the aerospace defense arena in Arizona. Our family of three made our first cross-country move from New York to suburban Phoenix. The only available option for me was a part-time staff pediatrician position at the Child Development Center & Arizona Children's Hospital. The work entailed seeing and treating patients who had developmental disorders. It was a hiatus in my pursuit for an academic and research career, but I enjoyed our relatively short-term experience in Phoenix, especially the weather. Although summer could be brutally hot during the day, it invariably cooled to very comfortable seventies in the evenings. Also, it almost never rained. In our early days in Arizona, when my license plate still read Massachusetts, a gentleman filling gas next to me commented, "You will love the weather here. Unlike Massachusetts, you can plan barbecue parties months in advance and not have to worry that it might be ruined by rain."

Our younger son was born in 1978, while we were in Arizona. A year later, in 1979, we made our second cross-country move back to the East Coast for new career opportunities. My husband was offered a staff position at one of the major aerospace companies in the greater Boston area. And I, working as a part-time pediatrician in Arizona at the time with no real challenges or chances to advance, had been idling and anxiously waiting for a suitable career path to appear. When the possibility finally dawned, we excitedly packed up and moved to Boston, the city that was to become the most dear to my heart.

Initially, though, the only available job I could find was a staff physician position at the Walter E. Fernald State School in Waltham, a city approximately thirteen miles west of Boston. Although named a "school," the organization was not a school in the traditional sense. It was an institution for people with developmental and physical disabilities. Along with five other physicians, I provided medical care to these patients. The job was not quite the academic career I had envisioned for myself, but I made the best I could out of what it was able to offer.

Located on the same grounds as the Walter Fernald State School was the Eunice Kennedy Shriver Center for Mental Retardation (Shriver Center in short). The founder was Eunice Kennedy Shriver (July 10, 1921–August 11, 2009), a graduate of Stanford University and a sister of the thirty-fifth president, John F. Kennedy. The Shriver Center was dedicated to researching mental disabilities. The Kennedy family had a mentally handicapped child, and Eunice Kennedy Shriver devoted her life for the cause of improving lives of individuals who were developmentally and intellectually disadvantaged.

After I completed my duties of taking care of the various issues of my patients at the Walter Fernald State School, I would spend all my free time, which was usually plenty, at the research arm of the Shriver

Center. I successfully collaborated with a researcher who was working on the mechanisms of various chromosome abnormalities. I also participated in the Shriver Center's weekly medical conference to keep up my medical knowledge. In fact, it was in one of the conferences that I first heard the term "fragile X syndrome" which, serendipitously, was to become one of my research topics a few years later.

The added activities at Shriver Center did not affect my primary work at Walter Fernald State School, and I was able to fulfill my duties adequately as a physician to all my patients at Fernald, which was what I was employed to do. That was when I had my biggest break. I was offered a research and clinical fellow position at the Massachusetts General Hospital (Mass General in short) with a joint appointment at Harvard Medical School. I had not dreamed of such a position; I had always thought Mass General and Harvard were beyond my reach. I owed this rather luminous career opportunity to my husband; it was only with his suggestion and encouragement that I pursued the possibility. In fact, it was not an announced open position when I first made a cold call and tried to explore the opportunity. Somehow, I was invited for an interview and was immediately asked to join this world-renowned organization. I was later told that a recommendation letter written by the laboratory director I worked with at Shriver Center included these words: "Grab her while you have the chance."

For three years, from 1981 to 1984, I was privileged to be on Mass General's academic roster as an instructor in pediatrics. I was able to pursue my true interest in research under the guidance of my mentor, Richard W. Erbe, MD, chief of the Genetics Unit of Mass General and an expert in folate (one of the B vitamins) metabolism. One of my research projects involved studying the relationship between folate deficiency and a genetic disorder named "fragile X syndrome." The commonly observed physical and mental abnormalities in patients with this syndrome included developmental delay and intellectual disability; physical features of large head, prominent forehead, large ears, loose joints, large testes; and behavior difficulties such as anxiety, aggressiveness, attention deficit, and hyperactivity. When chromosome analyses were performed on these patients' cells that had been grown in culture media deficient in folate, a break at one end of their X chromosome could be observed, hence the descriptive term "fragile X." This observation prompted us to ask whether low levels of folate could be a cause for the observed physical and mental abnormalities in patients diagnosed with this syndrome. We sought to study and compare folate metabolism in cells obtained from fragile X syndrome patients with cells from normal control individuals. Many experiments later, we were able to conclude that there was no evidence for an intrinsic defect in folate metabolism in these patients. Thus, treatment with folate supplement was not a viable therapeutic modality. We published our findings in the *American Journal of Medical Genetics* in 1984. It was one of the contributions to science that Dr. Erbe and I were able to deliver. While a minute step, that was how progress in science usually began.

The cause of fragile X syndrome had since been delineated. It resulted from an increase in the length of a gene named *FMR1* and was fully unrelated to either folate itself or folate metabolism.

My time at Mass General was one of the golden periods in my career. Immersed in the world-renowned research and clinical facility, I was given an opportunity to see patients with a wide range of genetic disorders, and I was able to spend most of my time working on research in the laboratory, which was my true passion. That arrangement suited me perfectly since I was basically an introvert who preferred solitude much more than interacting with people. Although my positions held during my long career in genetics frequently required me to give lectures and speeches, I had never felt very comfortable with public speaking.

With the publication of a number of rather consequential articles coauthored with Dr. Erbe in medical journals, I was fully rewarded for my efforts during the three years I was at Mass General.

* * * * *

In July 1984, my family made a third cross-country move; this time, it was from Boston to the Los Angeles area. My husband had accepted a job offer at the Aerospace Corporation in El Segundo, California. That move would prove to have a monumental impact on his luminous career and on our marriage.

Prior to our move, we went to the Los Angeles area to house hunt. The personnel department of the Aerospace Corporation had initiated assistance for our relocation and put us in contact with a local Realtor who identified a number of properties for us to consider in the cities of Woodland Hills, Malibu, Santa Monica, and Marina del Rey. Spoiled by the fond memories of our Boston home with one acre of land in an exclusive community, we were not impressed by any of the houses the Realtor presented to us. Further, all those homes were located rather far from El Segundo, my husband's new workplace. After much wasted effort, we were finally shown the beautifully alluring and uniquely exquisite gem of Palos Verdes, an upscale peninsula community consisted of four cities (Rancho Palos Verdes, Palos Verdes Estate, Rolling Hills, and Rolling Hills Estate) at the southwest tip of Los Angeles, extending into the Pacific Ocean.

Without any hesitation and with anxious excitement, we made our offer and quickly settled in our new home. Apparently, a peninsula address was one of the most sought-after properties in southern California. A June 1990 *Los Angeles Times* article titled "The Hill: Tale of Four Affluent Cities" chronicled a home in Palos Verdes Peninsula as "a terraced prow of land at the southwest tip of Los Angeles County that is rural by Southland standards and affluent by any standard."

The view, the air, the atmosphere, and the weather in this community of well-maintained homes were truly otherworldly. I had so loved Boston that I was quite reluctant to move away from it. Now the stunning landscape surrounding my new home in Palos Verdes was at least able to curb some of my nostalgia for Boston.

View from my window: Palos Verdes Peninsula and the ocean.

* * * * *

A suitable job opportunity was not immediately available for me in a part of the country I had not known until then. Temporarily out of work, I became a full-time mother, volunteered at my younger son's first grade class, and searched for job openings. Months later, as I was flipping through a directory of general clinical services, I unexpectedly came across the name of a private organization: The Genetics Institute. Without any knowledge of the scope of work of the organization, I made a cold call and inquired if it had by chance a position for an American Board of Pediatrics and American Board of Medical Genetics-certified pediatrician/geneticist. "Not really, we are not looking for people at this time, but why don't you come in so we can have a chat?" I went, and we chatted. And what a blessed decision I made! Thus began my lifelong career in cytogenetics, defined as the study of inheritance in relation to the structure and function of chromosomes. It was at the beginning of 1985.

That was the last move for my husband until his death in 2014. Before finally returning to the Los Angeles area at the end of 1994 and settling down for good, I had to make two more cross-country moves for my younger son's schooling.

CHAPTER 5

A CAREER IN CYTOGENETICS

Finding My Passion

While the path of my education was straightforward, the course of my career was quite a different story. Dictated largely by my husband's career direction, which determined where we lived and consequently what opportunities were available to me, my professional life fluctuated between clinical and research, patient and laboratory. After leaving Purdue, my first clinical work was an internship in Baltimore, Maryland, followed by a one-year postdoctoral research experience at Cornell University in Ithaca, New York. From then on, I explored various clinical and research endeavors in Long Island, Phoenix, Boston, Lexington, and finally back to Pasadena before settling down for good. I stayed in Pasadena until my retirement.

Desperately in need of a job in genetics after we moved to Palos Verdes, I visited the Genetics Institute at the beginning of 1985 without a clear concept of what was awaiting me. I had been told they had no job openings, but I accepted the invitation and paid a visit to learn the scope of the organization and its work. I drove the entire length of the 110 freeway from its southernmost end to its northern end and beyond. The Genetics Institute was located in Alhambra at the time, more than forty miles from Palos Verdes where my family resided. I met with the founder, Omar S. Alfi, MD, and his only associate E. Robert Wassman, MD. The organization's main focus was diagnosing chromosome abnormalities and genetic counseling for patients and their families, a subspecialty known as cytogenetics. I had limited exposure to this subspecialty during my training years in the field of genetics and had never considered it the focus of my career, but it was the only available option at the time—and I was willing to explore it.

What was expected to be simply a chat turned out to be a job offer. Somehow, Dr. Alfi saw my potential. Without waiting for reference letters from my previous mentors at Mass General, he decided to take a chance and offered me a part-time position on the spot. The terms were straightforward: "We will do it on a three-month trial basis. After that, we will either continue the employment with or without adjusting your salary, or we will not be able to retain you."

I took the "temporary" job without hesitation and began working immediately. On my first day, I came upon a case in which one of the number 2 chromosome pair appeared abnormal to me. I pointed it out. After reviewing the case, Dr. Alfi agreed with my assessment that there was a very small deletion (loss of chromosomal material). He was quite impressed that I was able to detect the abnormality. Within a month, my salary was doubled—and then tripled. I was enthusiastically welcomed to stay as a regular employee.

The part-time arrangement suited me perfectly. I dropped the children off at school, went to work, left work four hours later, drove in the notoriously heavy Los Angeles traffic back to Palos Verdes to pick up my sons from school, and then drove them to various sports and extracurricular activities before returning home. If I was stuck in traffic before mobile phones were popular, I had to exit the freeway, find a pay phone, and called my sons' school to inform the office I would be late picking them up. There were no alternatives at the time, for me at least. I maintained the part-time status until my sons were out of the house and away to schools—James to Phillips Academy in Andover, Massachusetts, and his brother David to Johns Hopkins

University in Baltimore, Maryland. It was the only period during my entire professional career that I stuck to a four-hour workday schedule. After both children were out of the house and I no longer had to get to their school at a prescribed time, I reverted back to be a what people described as "workaholic" with an average ten-hour workday.

* * * * *

Dr. Alfi was a person of faith, wisdom, humility, and unparalleled kindness. He had been the head of the Division of Medical Genetics at the Children's Hospital of Los Angeles in the 1970s. With his unique vision and courage, he left academia in 1981 to establish the Genetics Institute, the first private, full-service cytogenetics laboratory in the country.

Chromosome analysis and other genetic testing had been performed exclusively within university settings until then. Dr. Alfi singlehandedly changed that landscape. He understood the flawed inefficiencies, constraints, and red tape in academic institutions. Leaving academia and establishing a private genetics laboratory, he proved high-quality, cost-effective, and comprehensive diagnostic and management services for families suffering from chromosome abnormalities could be achieved in a private laboratory. Further, by personally working on the ingredients and compositions, he developed cell culture media that was able to more adequately support cell growth and thus allowed, for the first time, an average turnaround of prenatal diagnosis from fourteen days to seven days. This was an important aspect of prenatal diagnosis; it allowed earlier alleviation of anxieties in normal pregnancies and earlier intervention in cases where abnormalities in the fetus were detected. With superb quality and impeccable services, the number of incoming specimens increased and multiplied, and the Genetics Institute blossomed quickly.

Following the example of Dr. Alfi's pioneering vision, more and more private genetics laboratories sprung up across the country. We quickly realized that in order to avoid confusion with other genetics organizations, a designation more specific than the Genetics Institute was needed. A contest for such a name was run among all employees and Alfigen/The Genetics Institute (Alfigen in short) won the title.

Alfigen expanded rapidly and, in 1987, the laboratory was moved a few miles to a larger facility in Pasadena. It enjoyed the status of being among the first of many new technologies associated with chromosome analysis such as fluorescence in-situ hybridization (using a fluorescent dye tag to diagnose abnormalities too small to be detected with a regular microscope alone) and preimplantation genetic diagnosis and screening (diagnose and/or screen conceptuses for carrying abnormal number or abnormal structure of chromosomes very early in pregnancy before the embryo was implanted in the uterus). Later, testing for many molecular genetic diseases such as Ashkenazi Jewish genetic diseases screening and cystic fibrosis mutation analysis were also added to its menu. Throughout, Alfigen maintained its reputation as among the best private cytogenetics laboratories in the country.

Besides genetic testing, Alfigen also boasted to be the only private genetics laboratory accredited by the American Board of Medical Genetics to be a provider of fellowship training programs until the late 1990s when the Board no longer approved any of these programs outside of academic institutions.

Coincidentally—or perhaps as might be expected—according to the principle of "like attracts like," Dr. Alfi, Dr. Wassman, and I were all American Board of Pediatrics-certified pediatricians and American Board of Medical Genetics-certified geneticists in two subspecialties: clinical genetics and clinical cytogenetics. An institution, public or private, having a staff member with such extensive credentials was not common at the time, let alone all three of its doctoral members.

* * * * *

Before knowing chromosomes, I had not considered cytogenetics as a career choice. I loved genetics; learning about the segregation of maternally and paternally inherited genes in high school had piqued my interest. Exposure to the case of G6PD deficiency during my internship days and subsequently many other patients with genetic diseases also charmed me toward genetics. However, studying chromosomes, which could be visualized only with high-powered magnification, had not yet impressed me. To my ignorant mind at the time, they were only similar-looking bodies with dark and light bands of various sizes. Since individual genes that reside on chromosomes could not be seen or be characterized with microscopes alone, I naïvely presumed there was an element of arbitrariness involved in the science of cytogenetics; its scientific merit was not yet quite convincing for my narrow and limited mind. But once I stepped into the field and was forced to examine it carefully, I realized my misconception and discovered the beauty of the science. It became the center of my endearing lifelong career.

In normal individuals, there are twenty-three pairs of chromosomes in each cell. One set of the twenty-three chromosomes is inherited from the father, and the other set is inherited from the mother. Chromosomes are named from one to twenty-two, largely based on the size and pattern of their alternating dark and light bands along the length of each chromosome. The remaining pair is the sex chromosome that determines the gender of a person; females have two X chromosomes, and males have one X chromosome and one Y chromosome.

Chromosomes are composed of DNA and proteins; they carry the genetic codes that dictate the characteristics of an individual. Even small changes in its constitution can sometimes result in devastating consequences. In fact, many chromosomally abnormal embryos or fetuses cannot survive and are aborted spontaneously before they can be born. Sometimes the loss is so early in the pregnancy that the woman might not realize she has lost a pregnancy. The miscarriage rate in recognized pregnancies is roughly 10–20 percent, while the overall rate is estimated to be around 30–50 percent.

The most common chromosome abnormality is Down syndrome. These patients have three copies of number 21 chromosome in each cell instead of the normal two copies. Some common features of

Down syndrome patients include such physical characteristics as upward slanted eyes, flat nasal bridge, protruding tongue, small hands and feet, low muscle tone, short stature, and heart defects, which are present in approximately 40–50 percent of patients. Mild to moderate intellectual disability is nearly universally observed.

Chromosome abnormality can also involve its structure, even if the total number remains at the normal forty-six. One of the many examples of structural abnormalities is DiGeorge syndrome, also known as velocardiofacial syndrome, which is associated with anomalies of the face and heart, and may include other abnormalities such as cleft palate, feeding difficulties, developmental delay, and learning disability. This syndrome is due to a very tiny deletion—a loss of minuscule amounts of DNA—on one of the two number 22 chromosomes. Because the size of the deletion is smaller than a regular microscope can detect, a diagnosis requires additional special studies.

An example of a special study commonly employed to aid in the diagnosis of a minute chromosome abnormality is the *fluorescence in situ hybridization* (FISH) in which a sample of a patient's DNA is treated with a fragment of DNA of a known sequence that has been tagged with a fluorescent dye (the *probe*). The probe will hybridize with (bind to) the target DNA and produce a fluorescent signal that can be visualized with a fluorescence microscope. If a patient has a deletion of the region in question, chromosomes with deletions cannot bind with the probe, and the expected signal will therefore be absent.

More than 99 percent of our DNA is the same across the human race. The only 0.5 percent or so difference is sufficient to make one person different from all others. Except monozygotic twins, no two people have exactly the same DNA sequences.

Because of the uniqueness of each person's DNA and because DNA is passed on from parent to child, unexpected—sometimes embarrassing or unwelcome—family relationships such as nonpaternity may be detected during the process of performing either chromosome analyses or molecular DNA analyses on more than one member of the family. This can be illustrated by a case we encountered in our laboratory.

Amniocentesis was performed on a thirty-seven-year-old woman because of advanced maternal age. "Advanced maternal age" was commonly defined as mother's age being thirty-five or above at the time of delivery. In general, the chance of having a chromosomally abnormal child increases with increasing maternal age. At age thirty-five, the risk and benefit of performing the amniocentesis procedure to detect a fetal chromosome abnormality—and thus providing options for intervention to the family—outweighed the risk of the procedure itself. In this case, chromosome analysis performed on the amniotic fluid specimen revealed a coincidental finding unrelated to maternal age: the fetus had a balanced reciprocal translocation between one chromosome 3 and one chromosome 12. A portion of one chromosome 3 had moved to one chromosome 12 and a portion of one chromosome 12 had moved to one chromosome 3. This rearrangement was interpreted as balanced. It appeared that no chromosomal material was either lost or gained; they merely exchanged positions.

To aid in understanding the significance of this finding, we recommended chromosome analyses be performed on both parents to determine whether the translocation was inherited from one of the parents or if it occurred de novo, that is, happening for the first time. If de novo, there would be a small possibility that a submicroscopic gain or loss of chromosomal material occurred in the process (a gain or loss of a minute amount of material too small to be detected even with a microscope), increasing the likelihood of physical/mental abnormalities in the fetus.

Subsequent chromosome analyses of both parents were normal, indicating the rearrangement occurred de novo. The family was counseled accordingly and was given an approximate 5–10 percent chance that the fetus might be affected with some physical/mental defects.

Two days later, the woman came back to our genetic counseling department with another man and requested a chromosome analysis be performed on him. Not unexpectedly, the result showed he had the same balanced translocation as was found in the amniotic fluid specimen. With this additional information, we had to revise the original report and indicate that the translocation observed in the fetus was indeed inherited from the father of the pregnancy and therefore was of negligible consequence to the fetus.

We did not get involved in how the patients dealt with the information presented on the revised report. It was left to the families to decide their course of action.

Likewise, molecular genetic testing that was performed in our laboratory equally ran the risk of unexpectedly discovering an unwelcomed family relationship, including nonpaternity. Unveiling such information could be so destructive to the integrity of a family that it became a standard practice in all laboratories to include a disclaimer on all reports that read roughly: "Genetic testing may uncover an unexpected family relationship."

On the other hand, molecular testing has the power of discriminating and exonerating seemingly infidel family relationships. The first two such cases were reported in 1988 and 1989, when two independent reports were published in the *American Journal of Human Genetics*. Two children from two unrelated families had cystic fibrosis, a recessive genetic disorder occurring only if both parents were carriers for the defective *CFTR* gene on one of their two number 7 chromosomes, and both passed to their offspring the one that carried the defect. Testing showed that in both families, only the mother carried the mutation on one of her two number 7 chromosomes. The *CFTR* genes in both fathers were normal. Nonpaternity was therefore suspected in both families. With additional molecular studies of the families, it was determined that both children had inherited both copies of their chromosome 7 from their mothers, the one that had the mutation. This mechanism is known as uniparental disomy (UPD), literally "one parent, two chromosomes"—a child inherited both copies of a chromosome from one parent instead of the norm of one from the mother and one from the father. This discovery, a very rare event that does occur in nature, provided explanation how these two families could have children affected with cystic fibrosis; it exonerated the mothers in both families.

I stayed with Alfigen for four years until 1989. With increasing traffic in the Los Angeles area, the daily drive from Palos Verdes to Pasadena became more and more difficult for me. When I was contacted for an opportunity to be clinical director at the Division of Medical Genetics at Harbor-UCLA Medical Center, only fifteen miles from my home, I decided to accept it. I regrettably resigned from Alfigen and joined Harbor-UCLA, which proved to be an academically rewarding experience for me.

Two years later, in 1991, my colleagues and I at Harbor-UCLA reported in the same prestigious *American Journal of Human Genetics* another mentally handicapped child who had UPD resulting from a slightly different mechanism. Our report was among the first to show that, for some chromosomes, the genetic material of a person has to be inherited from both parents to ensure normal development. Since then, multiple cases of UPD involving various chromosomes have been discovered. Some, but not all, of these cases were associated with physical and/or mental disabilities.

* * * * *

In the early fall of 1991, I left Los Angeles for Boston because of my younger son's schooling. He had been accepted to the famed private boarding high school, Phillips Academy, in suburban Boston. I moved to Boston to be closer to him since he was only thirteen. I returned four years later, in 1995, when he was graduating from high school, this time to stay. I was enthusiastically welcomed back to Alfigen. In short order, Dr. Alfi made me the medical director and laboratory director.

Owing to the exemplary leadership of Dr. Alfi, the staff of the institute was very stable with long tenures and low turnovers. The few who left for higher salaries invariably returned after a few months when it became clear to them money was not worth sacrificing the caring and rewarding work environment they had become familiar with at Alfigen.

The laboratory had expanded tremendously while I was away in Boston for my son's high school education. The number of our incoming specimens had doubled, tripled, and quadrupled. Upon my return, my colleagues and I immediately began working on bringing up new tests for various genetic diseases, including many molecular tests and, notably, the laboratory portion of preimplantation genetic screening and diagnosis, which put our laboratory as the very first in the country to be approved by the New York State Department of Health as a preimplantation genetic testing provider. These tests were performed in vitro (outside of the human body). Briefly, the patient was given hormonal therapy to stimulate egg development. A number of eggs were then retrieved from the ovary by an embryologist and fertilized individually with sperm in laboratory dishes containing culture media, a process known as in vitro fertilization. The fertilized eggs were kept in separate culture dishes containing culture media that provided nutrients to the dividing embryonic cells. The cells continued to divide, from one to two, two to four, four to eight, and so on.

The eight-cell stage was usually achieved by day three after the in vitro fertilization procedure. At this time, one or two cells from each fertilized egg could be biopsied without harming the embryo, and the biopsied cells were tested for specific diseases the fetus was at risk for. For example, we would screen the fertilized eggs for cystic fibrosis if both parents were carriers for the disease. Embryos that were free of the disease could be transferred back to the woman's uterus. The test involved collaboration between two specialties: specimen preparation performed by an embryologist and specimen screening performed by a cytogenetics laboratory.

As if by design, our collaborator, the in vitro fertilization laboratory, happened to be located right across from Alfigen. The embryologist who prepared the specimen for testing would call us before he took the specimen and walked with it across the street to our laboratory. There was no delay in getting the precious specimens into our laboratory for testing, which was a great advantage.

Dr. Alfi remained actively involved in the operations of the laboratory. He almost always attended our weekly laboratory meetings. In those meetings, he would give us instructions on various topics in cytogenetics and life lessons in general. An example depicted the idea that sometimes the same matter could be interpreted in different ways by different people—and both could be right. He showed us the famous "Boring figure," named after the American experimental psychologist Edwin Boring, which is a drawing of a face. Staring at the picture, some of us said it was a young girl, and others said it was a witch.

Both answers were right; there were no wrong answers. Dr. Alfi showed us how sometimes the same matter could be viewed from different angles. He taught us not to stubbornly insist upon our own opinion, to be open, and to accept possible alternatives.

Dr. Alfi was also a brilliant cytogeneticist. In 1973, he reported and characterized a rare chromosome 9 abnormality, which became known as Alfi syndrome. In these patients, a portion of the distal short end of chromosome number 9 was missing. Patients with this chromosome abnormality, described as "9p-" (9p minus), usually have triangular-shaped heads, abnormal facial features, low muscle tone, and developmental delay/intellectual disability. Since Dr. Alfi's first report, additional cases have been discovered. According to the Chromosome 9p- Network, a nonprofit support group comprised of parents and caregivers of individuals diagnosed with chromosome 9p deletion syndrome, the rate of occurrence of this chromosome abnormality was very low at about one in fifty thousand births.

True to his humble nature, Dr. Alfi always spoke of the abnormality as 9p-, and we never heard him refer to it as Alfi syndrome.

* * * * *

In 2004, at the age of seventy-six, Dr. Alfi officially retired from his lifelong career in genetics. He kept a portion of the laboratory space and continued working on the technique of isolating the very low number of fetal cells that had appeared in maternal blood circulation. These cells, along with fetal DNA that had also appeared in maternal blood, would be good specimen sources for prenatal testing since the more invasive procedure of amniocentesis to obtain fetal specimen for testing would be circumvented.

Dr. Alfi also remained an active contributing member of the society. He and Mrs. Alfi established many philanthropic organizations and gave away much of their wealth for the betterment of the community. In the last years of his retirement, Dr. Alfi suffered from a chronic illness that affected his speech and gait, but he remained confident and positive. Never once did he resign to his fate. During his retirement, two of my colleagues and I visited him regularly. We witnessed firsthand the loving and mutually respectful interactions between Dr. and Mrs. Alfi. I was reminded of an adage: "Behind every great man is a great woman."

The news of Dr. Alfi's passing came to me on Sunday, June 4, 2017. I was attending a wedding at the Sherwood Country Club in Thousand Oaks, California. It was a gorgeous afternoon that inspired feelings of joy and thanksgiving; the breeze was gentle, and the sky was a pure blue without a single cloud. I sat in the beautifully decorated outdoor venue, enjoying and appreciating the charmingly serene sea of green in front of me while waiting for the ceremony to begin. My mobile phone vibrated gently. I looked down; it was the devastating message that Dr. Alfi had passed away. I was stunned and compelled to experience the mixed emotion of the joy of witnessing the beginning of a new life together of two people deeply in love juxtaposed with the profound sorrow, anguish, and grief for losing a beloved mentor who had given me my career and taught me to be a better person in so many ways.

Hundreds upon hundreds of mourners came to the funeral and memorial the next day. Dr. Wassman, whom I first met during my interview at Alfigen when it was still the Genetics Institute, arrived from Park City, Utah. Many others came from out of town at literally a moment's notice. It was a testament of how broadly and how deeply Dr. Alfi had touched lives.

Dr. Alfi left behind his beloved wife of sixty-two years, three children, eleven grandchildren, and three great-grandchildren. He preached love by example and regarded all with warmth and compassion. Loved by all members of his laboratory and beyond, he undeniably influenced many lives. My heart was filled with gratitude for having crossed my path, both professional and personal, with Alfigen.

* * * * *

The more recent discovery and development of the TALEN (transcription activator-like effector nucleases) and the CRISPR/Cas9 (clustered regularly interspaced short palindromic repeats coupled with the enzyme Cas9) gene-editing technology exemplified the potential to correct inborn errors at the gene level. These techniques would allow removal of DNA sequences that code for abnormal or defective proteins and replace them with normal sequences. Ethical and moral issues surrounding such applications were many, naturally, and would need extensive scrutiny and oversight.

Although fate turned my career direction to non-academia, I never abandoned my desire for research and teaching. In 2000, as part of Alfigen's efforts to provide services to the physician community, we started a quarterly educational "Update Series" on various topics in genetics, including "Genomic Imprinting and Uniparental Disomy" (a naturally occurring phenomenon demonstrating that certain genes can behave and function differently depending on whether they are inherited from the mother or from the father), "First Trimester Prenatal Screening" (using the level of naturally produced chemicals in pregnant women's blood to screen for pregnancies with a higher possibility that the fetus might be affected with Down syndrome or certain other abnormalities), and "Genetic Aspects of Cystic Fibrosis."

The Update Series was approved by the Accreditation Council for Continuing Medical Education (ACCME) as one of the continuing medical education activities eligible for CME credits. Such credits were one of the necessary requirements for physicians to keep their medical licenses active and valid. Through the years, I also maintained an adjunct faculty position at the California State University in Northridge. My colleagues and I taught courses on the subject of cytogenetics to genetic counseling students.

Our knowledge in science and genetics was leaping at a delirious pace. I was fortunate to have entered the field in time to experience its astonishing progress. It has been one of my ultimate satisfactions to be a participant of the great transformation in human genetics and witness the discovery and understanding of phenomena that had been present in nature all along.

Fate put me in contact with Dr. Alfi's Alfigen/The Genetics Institute, a private non-university organization. Yet, Dr. Alfi had his roots in academia and allowed me to approach my work as an academician. I had the best of both worlds; I was able to provide diagnostic services, and I was also able to perform research when opportunities knocked. While working at Alfigen, I published seven additional articles in genetics journals and wrote two chapters for a cytogenetics reference book. It was a career both treasured and rewarding.

More than sixty years had passed since the field of human cytogenetics took its first steps. It was in 1956 when the number of chromosomes in human cell was finally correctly determined to be forty-six. I was ten then, in the faraway land of Taiwan, oblivious of the field that was to become the center of my career more than thirty years later. I stayed in cytogenetics and never regretted turning my back on the much more lucrative field of clinical medicine. I am in awe as I look back at my incomparable journey in this fascinating field of cytogenetics.

* * * * *

After Dr. Alfi established the first private cytogenetics laboratory in 1981, many more private laboratories were founded to get in on the action in this exciting field that held vast promises and opportunities. With its reputation in quality and the ability to bring up new tests ahead of other institutions, suitors to acquire Alfigen were many. In 2004, twenty-three years after Dr. Alfi pioneered a private genetics laboratory, Genzyme Genetics, a biotechnology company based in Cambridge, Massachusetts, and named in 2006 and 2007 one of *Fortune*'s "One Hundred Best Companies to Work For," finally fulfilled its longtime desire and succeeded in obtaining Alfigen. I stayed with Genzyme Genetics and continued our efforts to maintain the highest quality of our laboratory. An additional transfer of ownership from Genzyme to LabCorp occurred in 2010. Then, in 2014, LabCorp was consolidated with its main laboratory in Santa Fe, New Mexico. Not wanting to move away to New Mexico from my home of nearly twenty years in Southern California, and since I had already surpassed my retirement age, I decided to retire and depart from my lifelong career in science.

As I ruminate over my more than thirty years of life dedicated to genetics, I like to think that I added a drop or two of truth to the infinite sea of knowledge. That, in my mind, justified my journey on this divinely constructed earth.

On Friday, August 29, 2014, as our laboratory in California was closing its doors for good, I packed up the more than thirty years of my life in cytogenetics, bid an agonizing goodbye to my daytime home of countless hours, and walked into retirement. That, serendipitously, took me to a second career I had not yet dreamed of: a return to my first love of literature and writing.

CHAPTER 6

FAMILY LIFE

There Is a Fountain

In the summer of 1990, my family took a trip to the East Coast to visit a number of college campuses in order to identify schools for our older son to consider. He would be starting college the following year. My husband suggested a side trip to Phillips Academy Andover for our younger son to consider; James would be ready to begin high school in the upcoming year when his brother David began college.

Phillips Academy Andover was a highly competitive and esteemed private boarding high school in Andover, Massachusetts, less than twenty-five miles north of Boston. The school was also simply referred to as "Andover." It was founded in 1778, at the height of the American Revolutionary War, by Samuel Phillips Jr. (1752–1802), an American merchant, manufacturer, and politician. It was the oldest university preparatory boarding high school in the country. Its alumni included such notables as Oliver Wendell Holmes Jr., former Chief Justice of the United States Supreme Court; Dr. Benjamin Spock, pediatrician and author of *Baby and Child Care*; former Yale President and baseball commissioner A. Bartlett Giamatti; actor Humphrey Bogart (expelled from Andover allegedly for assaulting the headmaster and throwing him in the campus pond); John F. Kennedy Jr. who was killed in an aviation accident in 1999 at age thirty-eight; former presidents George W. Bush and George H. W. Bush; and many more.

* * * * *

James was not too thrilled initially with the idea of attending a boarding school away from home, but he was immediately attracted by the alluring college-like campus. He applied, interviewed, and was accepted to the school, a rather celebratory achievement as the acceptance rate was in the low teens, similar to Ivy League colleges. So, in 1991, at the tender age of thirteen, he began high school.

To me, thirteen was too young an age to be completely out of the house and be on his own. I decided to move back to the Boston area with him while my husband stayed in California to continue his work at the Aerospace Corporation. In the meantime, our older son, four years older than James, chose to matriculate at the Johns Hopkins University in Baltimore, Maryland. The distance between Baltimore and Andover was more than four hundred miles, but it was much closer than if I had stayed in California and had to travel from Palos Verdes to visit them periodically. He would be able to come from Baltimore to our Boston home whenever he had a few days off from Hopkins. It was important since he was often homesick during his first semester of college. With a residence in Boston, he would be able to come home relatively often.

It was a good arrangement for us, and I immediately called the director and owner of a private organization, Prenatal Diagnostic Center, to see if he had a suitable position for me. I had known him while I was completing my training in genetics at Mass General; he was a junior faculty member at the time. While I had moved to California after my fellowship training, he had stayed in Boston. He subsequently left Mass General to open a private genetic services center providing amniocentesis, genetic testing, and genetic counseling services. He later told me that after hanging up the phone that day, he jumped up and down with joy and yelled, "My prayer has been answered."

He had been trying for some time to find the right person to run the laboratory portion of the organization for him.

The Prenatal Diagnostic Center was located in Lexington, Massachusetts—the place where the first shot of the American Revolutionary War was reportedly fired on April 19, 1775. "The shot heard round the world" is how the poet, essayist, and philosopher Ralph Waldo Emerson famously described the battle of Lexington and Concord, cities located fifteen miles northwest of Boston. The Prenatal Diagnostic Center provided both clinical and laboratory diagnostic services to patients whose pregnancies were considered high-risk—those in whom the risks of having an undesirable pregnancy outcome to either the mother or the fetus were higher than that in the general population. Examples of such risk factors included maternal age thirty-five and above (commonly described as "advanced maternal age"); women with existing health conditions such as diabetes and/or high blood pressure; maternal consumption of alcohol and/or cigarette smoking during pregnancy; and multiple gestation (carrying more than one fetus). While the director and owner of the Prenatal Diagnostic Center performed amniocentesis procedures and fetal ultrasound examinations, I took on the responsibilities of the laboratory co-director overseeing all laboratory tests, which included maternal serum screening and chromosome analyses of all types of specimens, including amniotic fluid, blood, and various types of tissue.

My work at the Prenatal Diagnostic Center was an extension of my work at Alfigen. I also developed new tests, lectured on various topics in genetics, and provided continuing education to the entire laboratory staff. Although a private organization, both the owner and I were Harvard/Mass General trained and academically oriented. We consistently maintained the quality of the center at the highest level. While there, I also published a number of articles in cytogenetics journals.

I stayed at the Prenatal Diagnostic Center until James finished up his high school education at Andover, and then we moved back to California.

* * * * *

Before moving back to Boston with James and starting my new job at the Prenatal Diagnostic Center, I took a trip to house hunt in the surrounding areas of my soon-to-be new workplace. A local Realtor took me around, but I did not find any of the properties she had identified for me adequate. I had fond memories of our previous home on Weatherbee Drive in the city of Westwood where we lived between 1979 and 1984. That house was a brand-new two-story, four-bedroom home in a community of single-family residences, and each had an acre of land. The houses were arranged strategically and attractively in irregular-shaped circles. I wanted something comparable to what I had been used to, not in size but in style and comfort.

The next day, I drove around and tried to find such a place by myself. I came upon a community that had an attractive monument at the entrance engraved with these letters: "Bishops Forest." I drove in. The ambiance changed as soon as I entered the community; a winding road led gently uphill before fanning out in various directions, large mature trees lined both sides of the road, birds were flying and chirping among the trees, and squirrels were playfully chasing each other around. Before my eyes appeared waves of gentle slopes with small clusters of four or five two-story townhouses scattered among well-manicured grounds filled with plants, flowers, and more trees. It was a conveniently located city dwelling in a very rural setting; it was quiet, peaceful, and alluringly charming. I knew immediately that was where my home would be. Two months later, my two sons and I moved across the country to our new home. They were very excited and pleased with our new "temporary home" in the Boston area, which would last only for the duration of their schooling.

* * * * *

On James's registration and move-in day, I took him to Andover. The campus was lively, filled with prospective first-year students and their families, but my heart was tenderly and unrelentingly aching. Standing aside and watching him register by himself rather tentatively as one of the youngest of his first-year high school class, I wondered how he would fare on his own journey without his mother by his side. After all, he was only thirteen.

After navigating around various stations and stops to complete the entire registration process, we went to James's assigned dormitory in West Quad North, a quiet residence building on campus nestled among trees and greens. His dorm housed eight students, all "Juniors," Andover's designation for freshmen; the other three high school grades were named Lower, Upper, and Senior. The student dorm was on the third floor. It had three large rooms, each accommodating two or three people.

A student from Texas had already arrived; apparently his parents were not able to afford travel expenses, and he came alone, on full scholarship. He and James connected immediately, both evidently relieved to see a peer. As James and I unloaded the belongings we brought from home, the student we had just met followed us around and asked questions ceaselessly. I was somewhat comforted knowing there would be friends around James.

The house counselor and his family occupied the first level of the building. The school placed much emphasis on the development of its students in all aspects: scholastically, intellectually, socially, and emotionally. Faculty members also served as house counselors. The counselors and their families lived on campus in the same buildings as their student counselees to enable constant interactions. I met with James's house counselor as part of the scheduled activities for the day. He had already read James's file and knew a number of things about him, including his allergy to peanuts. James, although the youngest among his peers, was rather socially mature and was later entrusted to occasionally babysit his house counselor's young child.

After a very productive meeting with the counselor and learning our mutual expectations, I lingered on campus before attending the dinner that had been arranged for all incoming students and their parents. When the day ended, I reluctantly left with a heavily disquiet heart filled with unease and worry for leaving James by himself. Stopping by the grocery store before reaching home, I suddenly realized I was to shop for food solely for myself for the first time in my life. I was so emotionally distraught that I restarted my car and drove home in tears.

* * * * *

I visited Andover's college-like campus of approximately five hundred acres every weekend. I either picked up James and brought him home for the weekend or just dropped off his clean clothes and took his soiled laundry home to wash. After having quickly integrated into his new environment, he sometimes preferred to stay at school on weekends and spend time with his friends. At times, he invited his friends from Andover to come home with us and spend weekends together. I also visited him whenever after-school baseball games were played either on campus or at Phillips Exeter Academy in New Hampshire, approximately thirty-eight miles northeast of Phillips Academy Andover. Both schools, with similar names, were elite New England college-preparatory schools and were considered the top boarding schools in the country. In 2018, Andover was ranked as the best boarding high school in America. The two schools—Phillips Academy Andover and Phillips Exeter Academy—were rivals in both academics and athletics. The sports teams played each other often. On these occasions, I would take off from work and drive to watch their games.

Andover also housed two museums on campus: the Addison Gallery of American Art and the Robert S. Peabody Museum of Archaeology. The Addison was one of my favorite places, and I visited whenever I had free time on campus.

* * * * *

James liked to write. While we were still in Palos Verdes, he enrolled in a residential summer camp program at the University of Redlands in Redlands, California, approximately eighty miles northeast of our home. Of the courses he took was a creative writing class. He did not always show me his work, but here is one I came across:

> You were driving a brand-new red sports car. Suddenly everything became wet. Slowly you opened your eyes ... his red tongue licking your face. You got out of bed, a ball of fur in your arms. In the kitchen, you poured a glass of milk. Immediately he jumped at it. Like a bolt of flash, you wonder what life would be like without him. You do not want to find out.

He was around nine when he wrote it. I was impressed with the way he handled the transition from dream to reality. As a child, he had once told me he wanted to teach history and be a writer—or play baseball and write during off-season. It neither surprised me nor alarmed me since I expected him to change his mind multiple times before reaching his ultimate destination. In the end, he took a career path fully unlike any of his childhood dreams.

Ironically, both of our sons were extremely allergic to cats. Once, while still in Palos Verdes, we set up a tent in our backyard to give them a simulated camping experience. A neighbor's cat came to get in the action. Both brothers began sneezing immediately, and we had to dismantle the tent. It was the reason we never had pets in our house. Somehow, though, they both "outgrew" it and are now able to keep pets in their own homes.

Recently, I came across an essay James wrote in 1991 or 1992 for his history class while at Andover. He titled it "Oppenheimer's War." Julius Robert Oppenheimer was known as "the father of the atomic bomb" and was the director of the Los Alamos National Laboratory during the development of the bomb. Part of the introduction of James's fifteen-page report read:

> The weather over the Alamogordo Air Base in New Mexico had cleared for the first time in over a week. At 4 am in pitch dark, J. Robert Oppenheimer could not see the 10,000-pound monster that he had created, sleeping quietly in its 100-foot steel tower. He had not slept the night before, but rather stayed up smoking,

coughing, and worrying. Now twenty minutes before detonation, thoughts raced through his mind. He thought of the two endless years he had spent laboring under the scorching New Mexico sun. He thought of his girlfriend, who, three months earlier, had swallowed 62 doses of aspirin and drowned herself in her bathtub. He thought of his $10 bet with a fellow scientist *against* the success of an atom bomb. Most of all, he thought of the Bhagavad-Gita, and its words "If the radiance of a thousand suns were to burst into the sky, that would be like the splendor of the mighty one." Twenty minutes later, a new sun, created in the image of man, would rise to illuminate the desert floor and all those who dared to witness its birth, and Oppenheimer would inevitably lose his bet. One more line would race through his mind: I am become death, the shatterer of worlds …

The paper was carefully researched and heavily referenced with multiple footnotes throughout. It was obvious James had spent much time, thought, and effort completing the assignment. At the side of his introduction page, his teacher wrote, "Vivid, eloquent, and effective introduction." The overall comment was: "An excellent paper. You make a convincing case: the paper has a clearly-defined thesis, a consistent line of argument, logical organization, and a base of evidence that's extremely well-chosen to prove your point. Your prose is lucid, smooth, and easy to read. You've done an impressive job of pulling material together from diverse sources into a seamless, coherent whole …" He received a grade of 5+ on a scale of 1 to 5.

When James was an infant, his father had been recruited and had begun working at the Los Alamos National Laboratory in Los Alamos, New Mexico, near Santa Fe. The organization was also universally known simply as "Los Alamos." It was where the atomic bombs were developed that ultimately ended the horrific World War II. My husband had arranged for me an unofficial interview there, hoping a suitable position might be available. Unfortunately, for an organization dedicated to science and technology, with its mission and vision: "To solve national security challenges through scientific excellence" and "To deliver science and technology to protect our nation and promote world stability," such an opportunity was not available at the time for a medicine/biology major like me. After waiting in vain for a few months, my husband decided to resign from the highly coveted position at Los Alamos, and we moved to Boston instead. I knew it was a huge sacrifice he made for me. On the other hand, he was so academically and scientifically astute; he would be able to succeed regardless of what organization he was associated with.

Not only intellectually advanced, James also had a good sense of humor. When we first moved to Palos Verdes, I took him to visit his new pediatrician. As part of safety instructions to all his new patients, the doctor told him to watch both sides before crossing streets. After the appointment, and as we were ready to cross the street, James looked up and then looked down, and said jokingly, "There are no airplanes, and there are no ants—we can cross now!" James had always been academically advanced, and he skipped third grade rather serendipitously. He was in a third and fourth grade combination class and was obviously performing above the third grade level in all subjects. His teacher recommended that he be grouped with the fourth graders. Concerned about possible difficulties in social adjustments due to his age, we were initially reluctant. However, the teacher felt he was socially more in tune with the fourth graders than the third graders. Then, when he was in fifth grade, he was intellectually ready to take high school math. In an essay he wrote as part of his application for admission to Andover, he included these paragraphs:

> As a fifth grader, I was looking forward to taking math class at the high school. Little did I know that the feeling was definitely not mutual.

The first day went by with no interferences. But that was the problem. For the first few days, no one spoke to me. It was as though their world was completely different from mine. Almost everyone was four years older, four years more mature. They know how to handle the situation.

It wasn't until another few days had passed before I had the courage to open my mouth and try to initiate a conversation. Once we started talking, it didn't stop. My age didn't seem to separate our friendship …

* * * * *

I too loved to write, and I had plenty of opportunities to do it during my long career as a cytogeneticist. Unlike routine blood tests such as CBC (complete blood counts) and urinalysis, many of the genetic tests performed in our laboratory required constructing customized reports that included narrative descriptions of results, their significance, and relevant recommendations for each patient. Extensive literature research for information of previously reported cases with similar findings was frequently needed to achieve such a goal. My colleagues liked my writing, and they frequently sought my input for reports they had to write. My mind had been completely consumed with scientific writing during my career days; I did not have the time or aspiration to write for leisure. Retirement had not been a vocabulary in my inventory until the day I learned that our laboratory in California was to be closed.

Shortly after plans to close our laboratory and consolidate it with the main LabCorp laboratory in New Mexico were announced and my decision to retire was made, the thought of reclaiming my lifelong love for writing crept back into my mind and unrelentingly tugged at my heart. I realized that—although dormant throughout all my days that had been consumed by my career—my desire for creative writing had not relented. I let the reawakening of my passion take me to a new horizon.

On the afternoon of my retirement, I sat down and began penning my first novel, the content of which was only beginning to ferment in my mind. I had no fictional writing experience and was ignorant of what I might encounter. However, almost immediately, I became completely absorbed in the story I was creating. I was so emotionally involved that I cried and laughed with the characters. I wrote day and night, every moment I had. I kept pen and paper by my bedside to jot down random thoughts that might appear stealthily and mercifully in my twilight state. Completely unprepared, I fell into a prolonged, unexplainable mood of melancholy, swinging high and low according to the words I wrote. I had not realized writing could be so emotionally draining, and I had never imagined I could be lost in my own creation. I also encountered frequent writer's block, clueless as to what was to come next. But invariably some message would appear in my head, and I would be able to continue moving forward. Nevertheless, I had to stop and rewrite almost constantly, sometimes entire paragraphs. Reading the book I had created, I was amazed by many of the passages and wondered how I could have conceived those ideas and thoughts.

I completed the work in five months and titled it *The Triumphant Life: A Story of Love and Courage.*

Eugene O'Neill wrote in a letter to his wife on their twelfth wedding anniversary:

> I give you the original script of this play of old sorrow, written in tears and blood. A sadly inappropriate gift, it would seem, for a day celebrating happiness. But you will understand. I mean it as a tribute to your love and tenderness which gave me the faith in love that enabled me to face my dead at last and write this play—write it with deep pity and understanding and forgiveness for all the four haunted Tyrones.

O'Neill's posthumously released *Long Day's Journey into Night* was a tragically powerful account of his own life, "written in tears and blood," he so stated. In his play, he had painfully and honestly recounted his dreadful personal experience. I do not remotely attempt to compare myself with O'Neill, but when writing *The Triumphant Life*, even though it was fiction, I too shed tears—and plenty of them.

* * * * *

During my growing years in Taiwan, we had very limited opportunities to attend concerts. Performances were few and far between. As I was preparing for my journey to the States, I realized such an opportunity might finally be in sight. I longed to see live concerts and operas on a stage. It was many years later before I was finally able to realize my dream. My sons had started taking violin lessons around the age of six or seven. Their violin teacher recommended that we expose them to opera. In 1985, we took them to see our first opera: the Los Angeles Opera's production of *Cosi fan tutte*. When James started high school at Andover and his brother started college at Johns Hopkins, I moved back to Boston to be closer to them. During school vacations, we went to see the New York Metropolitan Opera's performance of *Rigoletto*. The music, singing, acting, and set finally fulfilled my longtime wishes.

Since that first opera in New York, I have seen many more operas, plays, concerts, symphony orchestras, and art exhibits to fulfill my hunger for the arts. I also took James to the many live performances and various shows, dinner theaters, and concerts whenever he was off from school. To his credit, he was always willing to accompany me to those activities, which was not common for boys of his age.

To top it over, nature's charmingly distinct four seasons were proudly in display—the complete opposite of what I was used to in Taipei, Taiwan, where it was either scorching hot or freezing cold. There was no fall foliage or winter snow—only the gloomy rain that could pour anytime unannounced. Distinctions among spring, summer, autumn, and winter were always fuzzy in my hometown.

When I was caught in a sudden downpour while walking to class, I had to sit in the unheated (and un-air-conditioned) classroom, wet, shivering, and miserable.

I became aware of the true definition of four seasons only after I experienced life in the States. Purdue was where I saw snow for the first time. I ran out of my office, twirling in the falling flurry with sheer bliss. However, winter could be unforgivingly brutal, and heavy coats, hat, gloves, and boots added the misery of life. Yet, as noted by the poet Percy Bysshe Shelley in *Ode to the West Wind*: "If winter comes, can spring be far behind?"

The reawakening of spring ushered in narcissus, magnolias, lilacs, tulips, and more, a world full of colors. It was charming and inviting—not cold, not hot, just perfect—especially during April and May. Summer could be humid and balmy, in the eighties in July and August. Then came the exquisitely intoxicating autumn: rich, colorful, and abundant. Nature's luxurious paints of all shades lavishly swept through the entire region; waves and waves of trees of red, yellow, orange, pink, brown and beyond were interspersed here and there with soothing evergreens, topped over with reflections of nature's brilliant paints in ponds and lakes. It was enough to make one jump for joy. Then the chilly winter triumphed once again. It was an assurance that the seasons and the universe would continue on faithfully without fail for ages to come.

Autumn was also the season that brought me the saddest emotion. Early in the morning on a weekend, I went to Andover to visit James. He had decided to stay on campus to study for an upcoming exam. The campus was quiet; not another soul was in sight in that forestlike surrounding. I was alone, treading slowly step by step on the layers of fallen foliage and listening to the lonely echoes of the crushed dry petals and leaves under my feet. An overwhelming sentiment of solitude and insurmountable melancholy seized me without warning. Verses rose from the depth of my heart and formed a desperate plea.

Spring, the awakening of love, joy, and hope
Summer, the kingdom of the early morning ray

Autumn, the nature's color ablaze
Winter, the sorrow for what had gone astray

With an emotion beyond my comprehension, I began sobbing. No one was there to help wipe off my tears.

A lonely scene of fall foliage, Phillips Academy Andover.
Photo curtesy of Robert A. Dennis.

Winter, Phillips Academy Andover.
Photo curtesy of Robert A. Dennis.

* * * * *

Gradually I settled in and grew used to a life without my sons constantly by my side. I was now having more time to myself. When I volunteered at the Shriver Center between 1979 and 1981, I had become acquainted with the supervisor of the Shriver Center's cytogenetics laboratory. Now back to Boston in 1984, my Bishops Forest home in the city of Waltham was located quite close to her house in the town of Lincoln. We reconnected quickly and became quite close. A good cook, Mae invited me for meals often and visited me regularly. We usually sat by my bay window, talking about our work, discussing some of the interesting or challenging cytogenetics cases we encountered at our respective laboratories, and chatting about our lives and experiences in general.

I eventually broke down and began disclosing my emotional burdens in my marriage, which I had kept to myself through the years. We cried together over the despair and sorrow I had to face. Other than my mother, who had witnessed my anguish and suffering when she and my father took turns coming from Taiwan to help me taking care of the children, Mae remained the only person who was aware of the depth of that unspeakably dark period of my life.

After James graduated from Andover and was to start college in 1995, I moved back to the greater Los Angeles area to resume cytogenetics work at Alfigen. The children were no longer home, the reason for taking the long commute every day from Palos Verdes to Pasadena no longer existed. I began house hunting in and around the Pasadena area.

One Saturday, as I was driving around and hoping to find a suitable place to settle in, I came across a neighborhood in Glendale marked at its entrance by a very attractive monument engraved with these letters: Rancho San Rafael. It was a rather upscale private community.

I turned in and followed the winding road gently uphill. Opening before my eyes was an immaculately refreshing community of red-roofed, mostly white-walled houses, all with beautifully manicured yards. The houses were arranged in variously shaped rows along the wide residential streets. A clubhouse—complete with tennis courts, a swimming pool, and barbecue facilities—provided further attraction. It was like a quiet oasis perched above the bustling chaos of the city below. I had found my home. I knew immediately it was the closest place that stood a chance in comparison with my previous homes on Weatherbee Drive in Westwood or in Bishops Forest that I so loved.

Most houses in the community were two-story, four-bedroom homes. Even though I now had no need for a house that size, I knew it was the place I could call home. I jumped on it and found one with a commanding view from its backyard. A large and deep downward slope of groundcover and vegetations stood between the edge of my white-fenced yard and the faraway row of houses below. It gave me an unobstructed sweeping view that included a magnificent sunset nearly every evening, especially during the summer months when days were long—and I could sometimes be home from work in time to enjoy that splendid view. I sat in my backyard or in my evening retreat nook, watching the sky began displaying its brilliant colors—yellow, orange, gold, red, every color in between and beyond—until the last golden rays of the day turned deep red before bidding a final good night. That dazzling image of the glorious sky had been imbedded in my mind's eye.

And it was only seven miles from my workplace in Pasadena.

Brilliant sunset view from my backyard.
Rancho San Rafael, Glendale, California.

* * * * *

When I returned to Alfigen in 1995, I met a new colleague, a fellow art and literature lover who had joined the laboratory while I was in Boston. I was introduced to the technique of drawing and painting, skills I had never dreamed I could acquire. *Drawing on the Right Side of the Brain* was recommended to me and it argued that drawing is a process "so intertwined with seeing that the two can hardly be separated." In many ways, "teaching drawing is somewhat like teaching someone to ride a bicycle." You do not break down the technique of riding into small steps; you just get on the bike and go. I let go of my hesitation and took up a paintbrush, and a new horizon was beginning to dawn on me.

I began to draw and paint almost ceaselessly in my free time, in the evenings, and whenever I was not on call on weekends. I was so entrenched that I was frequently in the zone, an indescribable feeling that was both invigorating and exhilarating. James, on learning of my newly acquired interest, surprised me by registering me for a short drawing and painting course (four or five sessions) at the Los Angeles County Museum of Art as his 1996 Christmas gift to me. That course was my first and only formal exposure to painting techniques.

One of my drawings was a portrait of Dr. Alfi that I modeled from a photograph of him. He was very pleasantly surprised when I presented my drawing to him. Apparently, he also drew and painted when he was much younger. I had always considered Dr. Alfi a great geneticist, but I had never thought of him as an artist. Recalling a number of accomplished violinists and artists in my medical school, I was not surprised. It seemed like medicine and art go together.

My primitive drawing (oil pastel), after van Gogh, *Starry Night*.

My painting, oil, modeled after Edouard Manet, *Pinks and Clematis.*

* * * * *

On a late summer afternoon, I went to the beach city of Malibu approximately thirty-five miles from home. A friend had once taken me there. I was deeply stirred by the sharp contrast of the comfortingly soothing waves against a backdrop of chaotically busy city life. Various emotions—perplexing even to myself—agitated, boiled, and chased within me.

It was near dusk as I walked barefoot on the sand; the day had turned unusually cold, the sun had disappeared, and the beach was nearly deserted. I stood in solitude, staring at a motionless lone bird and listening to the sound of the rhythmic waves of the sea racing to shore repeatedly and unrelentingly. I irrepressibly sketched out the echo in my heart:

A lone bird in the center of the world,
So lonely, yet so grandiose,
The shore his stage, the sea his backdrop.

So tranquil, yet so vibrant,
The ocean unrelentingly beats its heart.

Like all great music, art, and literature,
The sound of the waves aches my heart.

And I am forever grateful,
For the beauty of nature,
And the ingenuity of human mind.

A lone bird on a late summer afternoon. Malibu, California.

* * * * *

One Saturday in the winter, I was on call and had to go to the office to review and sign out results of chromosome analyses, the technical portions of which had been completed by our laboratory technical staff. It was an unusually heavy day with a large number of cases, many of which had complex abnormalities. To provide meaningful reports to physicians who referred patients' specimens to us, I had to search for previously reported cases in the literature that had similar abnormalities. I synthesized all findings, composed detailed reports describing the results, and then proposed recommendations that also included any additional laboratory tests as necessary in meaningfully understandable language for the referring physicians who sent the patients' specimens to us. I did not finish my work until seven o'clock in the evening after nearly ten hours of nonstop work.

It was dark when I walked out of the building, alone and exhausted. In that empty and lonesome parking lot, I turned on the engine. The radio had been set at the NPR, and the host's soothing—and lonely—voice came on. "Stephen Foster was a nineteenth-century poet and songwriter. He wrote more than two hundred songs." He was talking about "the most famous songwriter of the nineteenth century." Foster, known as "the father of American music," was born in Lawrenceville, Pennsylvania, on July 4, 1826 and died on January 13, 1864, in the charity ward of New York's Bellevue Hospital, the oldest public hospital in the country. One of his most memorable ballads was *Beautiful Dreamer*. It was written not long before his death at age thirty-seven and published posthumously. Foster died penniless and in desolation. It was said that when he died, his purse contained less than forty cents.

Then the host played *Beautiful Dreamer*.

Beautiful dreamer, wake unto me,
Starlight and dewdrops are waiting for thee;
Sounds of the rude world, heard in the day,
Lull'd by the moonlight have all passed away.

Beautiful dreamer, queen of my song,
List while I woo thee with soft melody;
Gone are the cares of life's busy throng,
Beautiful dreamer, awake unto me.

The song depicted a lover, oblivious to worldly concerns, serenading a beautiful dreamer. Composed late in Foster's life, it became one of his most memorable ballads. The endearing lyrics, with what seemed to me its hauntingly sad music, tangoed together in that lonesome darkness of a nearly deserted road. It touched deeply my exhausted and already fragile emotions. My eyes misted. I pulled off the road and let my tears flow.

* * * * *

For a while, my husband would visit me in Glendale whenever he came from Palos Verdes to the Jet Propulsion Laboratory (JPL) of the National Aeronautics and Space Administration (NASA) in the city of La Canada-Flintridge, which was approximately seven miles northeast of my home. He had been working at the Aerospace Corporation in El Segundo ever since we moved from Boston to the Los Angeles area in 1984. JPL is one of the NASA centers that is a federally funded research and development center operated by California Institute of Technology (generally known as Caltech). My husband held an adjunct position at Caltech cooperating with other scientists working on issues surrounding rocket reentry among many other projects. Periodically, he needed to appear at the Pentagon for meetings on American space programs. He was extremely successful in the realm of science and had been involved in a number of NASA's space programs, including the Cassini spacecraft mission to Saturn. Named Asian-American of the Year by the Aerospace Corporation in 1996, he had received countless awards and commendations. His Delta II flowfield simulation had been on display at the Smithsonian Institute in Washington, D.C. along with at least one other collection I was aware of during the time we were together. He had also developed a highly accurate aerospace launch system code, which predicted the complex flowfield environment of a launch vehicle in flight. Dubbed a "world-renowned expert in computational and theoretical fluid dynamics," he had made his mark and contribution to the advancement of the American space program.

We remained married for many more years, but there had been many personality clashes that could not be easily reconciled, and disagreements exacerbated periodically without warning. The emotional and physical toll on me was indescribably heavy, and I presumed it was the same for him. It was not until our divorce in the year 2000 that I was finally able to begin living my life freely without fear of having to confront unexpected altercations. So many years later, I was finally at peace with myself and with the heartbreaking wound that had been inflicted on both of us by our tormenting relationship. And I believe he too finally realized that the gulf between us was too deep for reconciliation.

In a way, my husband and I were a mismatch. Perhaps we both were too proud, too self-centered, and too critical of each other. We were not able to accept the flaws we perceived in the person who was supposed to be our closest companion in life. Sadly, we robbed each other of the chance for an inspiring and invigorating marriage. It was an irreparable mistake and a true tragedy.

I never know what other people's lives are truly like behind closed doors, but mine was full of successes and failures. In my darkest days, I relied upon reading, writing, music, art, faith, and my work in genetics to mercifully give me solace, strength, and substance.

Chapter 7

TRIALS AND TRIBULATIONS

It Is Well with My Soul

It was the beginning of 1998, and I had just hosted my most popular and highly anticipated annual holiday party for our entire laboratory staff of more than seventy at my home in Rancho San Rafael. The party had become a tradition since I returned to Alfigen at the beginning of 1995. Everyone in our laboratory was still in the holiday mood, and chatters about the party were still heard in conversations.

I had been noticing some blood with my bowel movements for a number of months and finally made an appointment with a gastroenterologist at the beginning of the year. Without anticipating anything remotely alarming, I went to my appointment. I had only regarded it a routine visit with probably some benign lesion at the worst. However, after the examination and without waiting for results of any further laboratory tests, I was delivered the most unexpected and devastating diagnosis: colon cancer.

In an instant, the world mercilessly deserted me.

Working in the medical field, I had of course been exposed to patients who had cancer, but I had always subconsciously considered it other people's disease. Cancer had never been a meaningful word in my family. Other than my uncle who had been a smoker and died of lung cancer, none of my family members or other close relatives had had cancer. Further, I was only fifty-three then—the median age of colon cancer diagnosis was around sixty-eight. I was too young to have cancer. *No, that's not possible. There must have been a mistake.* I denied, I fought, I pleaded, and I begged, but the cruel reality forced me to accept it.

Surgery was scheduled immediately while additional tests and workups were being conducted. With fragile emotion and in constant gloom, tear, and confusion, I half-dreamingly had all my personal effects arranged, including hurriedly setting up a trust and a will. My first priorities were my sons. Both of them were still in school—my older son in medical school and my younger son in college. I sought my sister's help and asked her to arrange for continued financial support for them.

The emotional and practical support from Dr. Alfi, my associates, and my laboratory staff smoothed the ghastly process. I was told to take as much time as needed from work and to let go of any work-related responsibilities, but the psychological burden was heavy, and the emotional anguish was deep beyond consolation. I was seized with persistent sadness and unrelenting desperation.

There were a number of first-rate cancer centers in the greater Los Angeles area. A good friend, one of my MD colleagues, accompanied me to appointments for second opinions. She asked questions and took notes for me. After much discussion, debate, and consideration, we decided to seek care at City of Hope, a leading treatment and research center for cancer and other chronic life-threatening diseases in the city of Duarte, which was not too far from my home.

The tumor was localized, and treatment was considered to be a rather common and straightforward surgical procedure to remove the cancerous tissue. I was told to expect a five-to-seven-day hospital stay for the entire process. I ended up remaining in the hospital for nearly a month. I went in on Monday, January 26, 1998, and surgery was performed the next day. I was reluctantly discharged, actually against medical advice, on Saturday, February 21, 1998. I had been in the hospital for twenty-seven days.

My surgery was unexpectedly plagued with extensive complications. It was like Murphy's Law but amplified by a thousand: anything that could go wrong went terribly wrong. Initially a single laparoscopic port in the lower abdomen was made, and surgery was performed through the port. That was the typical "minimally invasive" procedure for un-metastasized colon cancer as was in my case. Unlike a traditional multiport laparoscopic approach, with this technique, only a single incision was necessary. This approach would leave only one small scar, and recovery after surgery was generally faster and less eventful. Unfortunately, unexpected complications during surgery changed the entire dynamics.

According to the operative report I later obtained, the tumor was easily movable, was not attached to the surrounding tissues, and there was no evidence of metastases. A relatively simple and straightforward surgical procedure was expected and planned. However, various complications during surgery soon became evident. It began with heavy bleeding that prompted surgeons to first extend the incision line and—when that proved ineffective—adding additional incisions in an attempt to find the source of the bleeding. Eventually it became necessary to convert the procedure from minimally invasive to a traditional open procedure to finally bring the bleeding under control. The entire surgery took much longer than anticipated, and the subsequent lengthy recovery was filled with unrelenting complications. I remembered the harrowing pain that threw me into an uncontrollable shriek while I was finally being wheeled back to the ward.

What followed was an unusually long and protracted postoperative course with multiple complex and agonizing difficulties. A partial bowel obstruction soon developed, and instead of resolving gradually and spontaneously with conservative management as it should have been, it progressed within days to complete obstruction. During this period, a nasogastric tube was inserted through my nose to my stomach to continuously suck out my stomach contents. I lay on my hospital bed, miserable and hopeless.

My sister Grace, sitting by my bedside, listened with me intently to the hissing sound made by the suction device. Suddenly the sound stopped. We looked at each other, almost rapturously, imagining the obstruction had cleared, but the merciless sound soon resumed. Eight long and dreary days after the original surgery, in an already extremely exhausted and weakened state, I was taken back to the operating room for a second surgery to release adhesions in the abdomen that had developed and which were apparently the cause of the bowel obstruction. I was told it would be a quick procedure to nip what was considered only a few adhesion sites. I remembered looking up at the wall clock before I was put under general anesthesia.

When I woke up, it was many hours later. Apparently there were unexpected massive dense adhesions involving the entire abdomen. "There was one proximal mucosal tear (mucosal layer is the innermost layer of the intestine); there were approximately seven different serosal tears (outermost layer of the intestine) along the mid portion of the jejunum, extending down the proximal ileum," the operative reports read. Further, in the process of attempting to release the adhesions, more tearing of the intestinal wall occurred, which required additional repairs. With the two gruelingly complicated surgeries— both were unfortunately associated with extensive complications— my abdomen suffered perpetual hardening, and my bowels have still not completely returned to normal.

Turning in bed and changing positions became formidable tasks. I was not able to move by myself and had to be turned by my caregivers. I also had to be propped up fully to stay in position. I lost control of my own body and became completely dependent on others. Those tasks that had always been automatic—and which I had always taken for granted—shouted loudly at me for attention. They demanded my acknowledgement for the mercy and grace I had been granted so freely without having to beg.

Recovery from the two lengthy and complex operations was exceedingly protracted, and the pain and discomfort were unrelenting. I was not allowed to eat because my abdomen stayed stubbornly silent, a sign of a lack of normal peristaltic movements of the intestines. With the bowel on strike, I had to be kept on intravenous fluids with absolutely nothing by mouth for more than three weeks. During mealtimes, I would look out from my hospital room window to watch people walking by with food trays in hand. I yearned to eat. Never had I imagined that being able to eat was such a privilege.

Worse, day after day and night after night, I was not able to fall asleep. Time went by very slowly in the hospital. Too slowly. I counted seconds, minutes, and hours, wishing and begging the next moment to arrive sooner. One by one, I watched enviously as other patients with the same colectomy procedures were admitted and then discharged; only I remained. I was dejected; there was no foreseeable prospect of going home for me.

Nurses and my loved ones asked what they could do for me. I had no answer. I only wanted to have my health back. But could they do that for me? I felt helpless. I sank into the darkest abyss, and I lost my hope. "Healthy" seemed like a mirage for me. I wondered if I would ever regain my health and be independent again. I was so miserable that I once lost my temper with my sister Ling. She was taking care of me one evening in the hospital, and I flew off the handle when she failed to immediately grasp what I wanted her to do for me. Sorrowfully, she murmured, "I am very tired too." A mixed emotion of shame and helplessness hit me like a rock. I swallowed my tears.

* * * * *

Thinking back, the warning signs had been present for almost six months. There had been sporadic rectal bleedings, but I had no loss of appetite or loss of weight. I had been as active as always. I ignored it. When I was told of the diagnosis, my reaction was typical: "Are you sure?" I could not accept it. It was not possible. Not cancer. Not me!

I never asked, "Why me?"

My brother Shenandoah brought me a cassette tape recorder and tapes to help me relax. I listened to "Give Thanks with a Grateful

Heart" over and over every night, all night; it did not put me to sleep, but it gave me peace:

Give thanks with a grateful heart
Give thanks to the Holy One
Give thanks because He's given Jesus Christ, His Son.

And now let the weak say, "I am strong."
Let the poor say, "I am rich."
Because of what the Lord has done for us.

Give thanks.

The song was written in 1978 by Henry Smith who suffered from a degenerative disease that later left him legally blind. It became one of my most favored hymns.

* * * * *

My two sisters, Ling and Grace, and my sister-in-law Agnes took turns to stay with me and cared for me during the entire time I was in the hospital, day and night, around the clock, without fail. There was not a single day or night I was left alone—except one morning toward the end of my hospitalization.

Ling lived in Northridge and worked evening shifts in Santa Clarita. Every night after work, she would drive the forty-five-mile distance directly to Duarte to take over the care for me. One morning, she asked if she could go home to take a short rest, clean up, and do a few chores before coming back. I would be told later that she left me that morning and, instead of going home to rest, she drove directly to Cedar-Sinai Hospital to visit my mother who had been hospitalized for respiratory failure as a result of idiopathic pulmonary fibrosis, a chronic disease with gradual scarring of the lung tissue without a known cause and without effective treatment. My mother had been fighting this long and unrelenting illness for more than five years, coughing off and on, sometimes protracted to the point she would wish to die and be relieved of the misery. This time, the coughing spell was so severe that she had to be hospitalized. I was not told of her condition until after I was discharged from the hospital.

My mother did not get out of the hospital; she passed away shortly after I was finally discharged and was struggling to get back on my feet. I was able to visit her during the last days of her life. She had looked at me lovingly and said, "You look good. I am glad." I recalled the time so many years ago when I was in my last year of medical school in Taiwan. She came to see me and gave me that beautiful necklace as a graduation gift. She had said, "You have never made me worry, emotionally or financially." After my mother's passing, I was told that on the day of my surgery, she paced back and forth continually in the hospital hallway in visible agitation and agony. I realized how much she had been worrying about my cancer. I wept.

A hymn rose in my heart, "It Is Well with My Soul," words written by Horatio G. Spafford and music composed by Philip P. Bliss. Spafford was a prominent American lawyer and a church elder. He lost all his daughters in a shipwreck on November 22, 1873, when his wife and their four daughters were sailing to Europe for a vacation. Spafford had stayed behind to take care of some unexpected last-minute business matters; 226 people lost their lives in the wreck. His wife was one of the forty-seven survivors. After she was rescued, she cabled her husband: "Saved alone." Spafford, on his voyage to join his wife immediately following the tragedy, comforted himself with those words, "It is well; the will of God be done." He later wrote his famous hymn based on those words.

When peace like a river, attendeth my way,
When sorrows like sea billows roll,
Whatever my lot, thou hast taught me to say,
It is well, it is well, with my soul.

Though Satan should buffet, though trials should come,
Let this blest assurance control,
That Christ has regarded my helpless estate,
And hath shed His own blood for my soul.

It became one of my most favored hymns.

* * * * *

My older son David and his wife Judy were both in medical school at the time, and they flew 2,700 miles from the East Coast to visit me. My daughter-in-law was pregnant with my first grandchild at the time. My younger son James arrived from San Francisco. He was in great distress; the news of cancer happening to his mother was beyond comprehension for this then not quite twenty-year-old young man who had barely begun adulthood. My husband, although we had been keeping separate households, also visited me and pledged to pay the patient portion of the astronomical medical bill.

I spent twenty-seven miserable and hopeless days in the hospital. With my insistence and pleading, I was finally reluctantly discharged to my sister Ling's care. My bowel had not yet returned to normal—it never would, unfortunately—and I was still in unrelenting pain and discomfort. In a much calmer and more relaxed environment, I was able to begin taking small steps toward recovery. I slept, I ate, and I walked around in the house as much and as frequently as I could. I was gradually nurtured back to health. My brother-in-law is a good cook; he tirelessly prepared the recommended diet for me and made sure my journey to recovery was smooth. Leaving all worries about work behind, it was a fully pampered period of my life. I stayed with them until I was able to go home and go back to work.

On March 16, 1998, fifty days after my initial surgery, I returned to work. A large well-crafted banner inscribed with "Welcome Back, Dr. Wang!" awaited me. The entire laboratory staff organized a schedule among themselves to take turns bringing food for me to ensure I was fed every day. For months, I was spared the burden of cooking. I was utterly humbled.

The same caring process for me repeated itself years later when my second husband Darrel passed away and left me alone.

* * * * *

But my fight and struggle against cancer had not ended. Although no lymph nodes were involved, the tumor was large and had infiltrated deeply into the entire thickness of the intestinal wall. For these reasons, adjunct treatment with chemotherapy was recommended, and I was forced to endure the hellish experience of the treatment—an experience I would never wish upon anyone, friend or foe. On the days of my scheduled appointments, I went to work in the morning, left early in the afternoon, drove eleven miles to City of Hope, receive the intravenous anti-cancer medication, and then drove seventeen miles home.

The side effects of chemotherapy were extremely debilitating and exhausting. I was seized with constant nausea, sometimes vomiting, loss of appetite, diarrhea, weakness, mouth sores, and overall exhaustion—a constellation of side effects I had been forewarned but did not truly understand until I was forced to experience them. It was so horrific that I was ready to give up, stop all treatments, and accept defeat. But my oncologist prodded me along relentlessly; she encouraged me, found ways to sustain my hope, modified the treatment regimen, and adjusted down the dosage of the medication to make it easier for me to tolerate. Still, I dragged and resisted. My emotions were raw and fragile. Whenever I had to wait slightly longer than usual for the intravenous drip of medicine to begin, I would complain about not being promptly attended to. At times, I would burst out crying with the tiniest perturbation. Nurses tried to comfort me, but I was usually hard to please. I had freely let my vulnerable side shown, which was quite unlike myself in normal times.

But all things must pass, regardless of how we receive them and how we deal with them. I had cried, I had fought, I had complained,

I had begged, and I had lost hope and perspective. In the end, I completed all three gruesome rounds of chemotherapy. There was light at the end of the tunnel!

The needle was finally removed from my arm for the last time: "It's over!" I can still taste the exhilarating bliss I felt at that moment. All the follow-up tests had been normal since, and I was declared cured. People described me as strong and courageous, but I knew I was carried forward by the love and care of so many people around me. The world did not desert me.

Morris B. Abram, a lawyer, the founder of UN Watch, and once the president of Brandeis University said, "We must begin to comprehend that death is not always to be fended off … During my treatment, I reflected that death is the frame around the painting of life. A painting on a canvas of infinite size, worked on eternally, would be without focus, meaning, and probably without beauty. A painting, as life, needs limits … I believe death to be the final and perhaps greatest teacher …" Abram died in 2000, twenty-seven years after he was treated for acute myelocytic leukemia.

The cancer experience changed my view and my outlook on life. I knew I could not live only to stay alive. Life is a gift, unearned and undeserved. There is much more meaning to life than just being alive. I must treat it with deep respect and gratitude. Our days on earth are a two-way process: give and take, bestow and receive, accommodate and compromise. I became more open, more tolerant, more generous, more considerate, more sympathetic, more perceptive, more determined, and hopefully more sagacious.

CHAPTER 8

REDEMPTION

Unanswered Prayer

In time, I met a friend seven years older than I who was to become my second husband. What a heavenly blessing it was! I felt safe, and I felt liberated. No longer did I need to be wary of making unintentional blunders that might ignite a prolonged and painful confrontation. It was refreshing to be able to freely express my thoughts and opinions.

Darrel's childhood was the complete opposite of mine; it had been filled with miseries beyond what I could ever imagine. His mother died before he was ten. He would never be able to forget the pain and desperation inside him as he watched his mother's body being taken away. Burning with anger and despair, he perceived her death as a desertion of him. This he related to me in tears after more than fifty years had passed.

His father remarried, and his stepmother treated him with unexplainable vengeance. In the bitter cold winter in the small town where he was born, Chillicothe, Ohio, she would put him out without a coat, letting him in only just before his father would get home from work. For years, he was starved and beaten. He kept his misery to himself, sparing his father the cruel reality. His childhood experience reminded me of a book I read many years before: *A Child Called It*. In the book, the author described how he was brutally treated by his own alcoholic mother as an "it" rather than a human being. How people could regard their own flesh and blood as their hated and despised enemy was utterly unfathomable; home was supposed to be a place where children were protected from outside elements. In the end, on her deathbed, Darrel's stepmother finally expressed remorse for having mistreated him. Darrel was able to forgive, but he would never be able to forget those horrifyingly dark days of his youth.

Growing up in Taiwan and witnessing the fact that all my friends and playmates attended school from kindergarten through at least high school, I had regarded education an unquestionably entitled privilege—and an obligation—for all children. Students who ended their formal education at the end of high school had usually failed to secure a place in the highly competitive college entrance examinations and not because their family could not afford the expenses. Costs of college in Taiwan were generally quite low, especially for the first-rate public schools.

For Darrel, education was a luxury. His schooling was frequently interrupted, sometimes for long periods of time. He had to work in the fields to help support his family. His hands and fingers were continually cracked in those icy Ohio winters. During the war, he enlisted and served in the air force as noncombat support personnel. With all the distractions, he somehow managed to work through college, obtaining a bachelor of arts degree at age thirty-one from Lincoln Christian College in Lincoln, Illinois. That was in 1970, the same year I graduated from the medical school of National Taiwan University with a medical degree and came to this country, fully oblivious of what was in my future. I was twenty-four then.

Against all odds, Darrel grew up a hopeless optimist—always positive, always upbeat, always kind, always giving, always forgiving, and always accepting trials and tribulations without complaint.

* * * * *

Like his father, Darrel was endowed with the gift of music. He could sit down at the piano and compose a new piece almost instantly: music, lyrics, and all. His music career, in the style of gospel, rock, and country, began in his early twenties. He formed a band with his friends, and they performed in clubs and on local radio stations. He was the lead singer and guitarist. Later, he recorded a compact disc of songs he wrote and sang. It was one of the few possessions he left me before his passing in 2009.

Darrel was equally a very gifted minister. He had been asked to preach Sunday services, both at the college and at a neighboring church when he was still a student at Lincoln Christian College. It was an honor not given lightly to undergraduate students. Moreover, his interests and strong background in psychology, his unwavering compassion for others, and his innate communication skills made him an ideal counselor to those in need. He would never let an opportunity slip if he could find a way to ease the burden of a troubled soul.

Darrel also developed a close relationship with my father. In 1999 at the age of eighty-seven, my father underwent a major cardiac surgery to repair an aortic valve that had not been functioning properly. His heart valve that controlled the path of blood flow had allowed some backflow into his heart with each heartbeat, a condition described as aortic insufficiency (also known as aortic regurgitation). This defect added much strain to his heart and caused weakness, shortness of breath, irregular heartbeat, and overall malaise. The only possible treatment was surgery to replace the improperly functioning heart valve with an artificial one obtained from pig or cow. The decision to undergo this risky surgery for people of his age was not made easily.

After extensive discussions and multiple consultations with his cardiologist and cardiac surgeons at Cedars-Sinai Medical Center, my father chose to proceed. He had decided that the benefits outweighed the risks, and he was willing to take his chances, anticipating a better quality of life if surgery proved successful. Surgery was successful, but the postoperative recovery from the brutal physical insult for people of his age was substantial, and he was in unrelenting pain and discomfort.

During the weeks of his long road to recovery, whenever we visited him in the hospital, Darrel would sit at his bedside and use mental imagery techniques, with me translating, to help ease my father's discomfort. Darrel would also wander about to other patients' rooms, strike up conversations, and provide subtle counseling and encouragement to any patient he came into contact with. He became a popular figure among patients and was, remarkably, welcomed by the nursing staff. He was able to maintain contact with a few of those patients throughout his life. He also became very close to my father.

After my mother died in 1998, my father did not want to move in with any of his four children and preferred to live by himself. Before we were finally able to find trusted live-in help to take care of my father, Darrel would often go visit him for me. Despite the language barrier, they somehow managed to understand each other and developed a close relationship. My father enjoyed a healthy life for eight more years after his open-heart surgery.

In his retirement, Darrel put his people skills to work. He volunteered his time and innovatively organized a clergy program for the sheriff's department to provide support and counseling services to sheriffs, deputies, and local families facing such catastrophic events as death, suicide, and major illness. The clergy volunteer group carried pagers and took turns responding to desperate pleas for help from families in the community.

Once, Darrel's pager went off in the middle of the night. He responded to the call, got up, and left. It was early afternoon when he finally returned in visible pain and dejection. An elderly couple had committed suicide; their bodies were found in the back of a small shopping mall. Darrel had spent most of the day counseling their surviving family members. He said to me, "The world has too much pain. We need to teach people how to have faith and look beyond. There is light at the end of the tunnel; it's not a cliché."

* * * * *

During his years in the Air Force, Darrel had been moved around the country, but he had never been in Boston, my most cherished city. When I was given the opportunity to go on a business trip to Boston in the late summer of 2009, he went with me and visited the city while I was in meetings.

Our laboratory in California had been acquired by Genzyme Genetics, and Genzyme's main laboratory in Boston was attempting to bring up a new test. I was asked to travel there to assist and oversee the successful completion of the project. While I was in meetings, Darrel took city tours and learned the history and character of the great city. For the first time, he experienced the rich history and culture of Boston.

We stayed a few more days after my meetings were completed, and my purpose for taking the trip was successful. Together we toured the campus of James's alma mater, Phillips Academy Andover, and we visited Harvard, MIT, and Mass General—those academic centers I had either been a part of or had a relationship with. I also introduced him to many of the historic sites and attractions in Boston and other parts of Massachusetts: the Museum of Fine Arts; the JFK Library; the famed Walden Pond where the nineteenth-century poet and philosopher Henry David Thoreau had built a log cabin and lived in solitude for two years; Faneuil Hall, a historic marketplace and meeting hall; Plymouth Plantation, a living-history museum; Cape Cod, a geographic cape extending into the Atlantic Ocean from the southeast corner of mainland Massachusetts (a cape is a large piece of land that sticks out into the sea from the coast); Martha's Vineyard, an island south of Cape Cod near the southernmost part of Massachusetts; and many other historic sites in Massachusetts.

Darrel was so impressed that for quite some time after we returned from the trip, he continued talking about his experiences. Boston's overall scholarly milieu had been metaphorically demonstrated by what Mark Twain once wrote: "In New York, they ask, 'How much money does he have?' In Philadelphia, they ask, 'Who were his parents?' In Boston, they ask, 'How much does he know?'"

Thoreau Cabin in Concord, Massachusetts, where Henry David Thoreau, a philosopher and naturalist, lived in solitude for two years.

* * * * *

For much of his adult life, Darrel suffered multiple medical and surgical complications. Years before we met, he had developed thrombosis in his upper leg. The skin over his thigh reddened, and he was seized with excruciating pain in and around the affected area. The diagnosis was not made immediately, and treatment was much delayed—a clear failure on the part of his physicians. Eventually, due to lack of blood supply, the area became necrotic and had to be surgically removed. These extensive and complex complications had left him in nearly constant pain over his back and legs ever since. He was able to largely ignore and suppress the misery and maintain a positive outlook for life: always pleasant, always willing, always accepting, always optimistic.

One early afternoon a few months after we returned from Boston, Darrel called me at work. I picked up the phone and heard him shrieking and moaning. A penetrating abdominal pain that even he was not able to withstand had suddenly seized him. He had already dialed 911 and was being taken by ambulance to the hospital. The pain was controlled by heavy analgesics, and he was able to carry on a conversation with me and his two sons when we visited him.

X-rays showed some possible free air in the abdomen. Other than pain control, though, no diagnostic or interventional attempts were made, and the surgeon decided to put him under observation for the night.

Early the next morning, I called the hospital to check on his condition and was told by the nursing staff that he was sleeping. I got up and went to the hospital to see him. As I walked in his room, I immediately noticed that his urinal was empty—and no entry had been made on his intake-and-output sheet. Apparently neither the nursing staff nor the surgeon on call that night had realized the seriousness of his condition. He was in septic shock: a life-threatening condition with persistent low blood pressure induced by overwhelming infections. I sounded the alarm; it was only then Darrel was hurriedly transferred to the intensive care unit. While he was being admitted, he opened his eyes and mouthed an inaudible "I love you" to me. He then closed his eyes. He never regained consciousness afterward and passed away a few hours later as a result of a perforation of the bowel, which caused extensive infection and acute renal failure. He was seventy-one.

I knew without a doubt that the nursing staff and the surgeon on call that night failed to properly monitor a seriously ill patient. Darrel's rapidly worsening condition during the night should have been noticed and realized had he been properly cared for. I had every right to bring a lawsuit against the hospital, but what would that do to a life that had already been lost? I recalled the incident some fifty years ago when my little brother drowned. Despite their heartbreaking pain and sorrow, my parents never once blamed his wet nurse. They were fully aware nothing could bring my brother back. Now, I know what Darrel would have wanted me to do. So, instead of a lawsuit, I sat down and wrote a letter to the head of the hospital's surgical department detailing the incident and describing the failure of their staff to adequately monitor and care for a critically ill patient. My hope was that a corrective action would be implemented to avoid another tragedy happening to a precious human life.

Darrel's passing came so suddenly and so unexpectedly. It took me a long time to adjust. Even though my mind knew I should accept the tragedies life dealt me, my heart was nonetheless weak and filled with grief. I waited for healing that time might mercifully bring.

With my husband, Darrel, in our happy days together.

* * * * *

Although I loved my Rancho San Rafael house, and it was in a very safe community, I had become less "brave" as I grew older. With Darrel no longer by my side, the house felt too big for me alone. When occasionally my doorbell rang at night, I would be so scared and disturbed that I froze—even though it invariably turned out to be either children trying to sell candy and cookies as fund-raising activities for their schools or the occasional campaign effort by people running for seats on the board of our homeowners association.

I decided to downsize and began searching for smaller homes in more intimate settings. I spent much of my free time on weekends looking in and around Pasadena where my workplace was located. Eventually I found a place in a city close to Pasadena. It was a brand-new community within a newly built outdoor shopping center in the heart of Glendale, called Americana at Brand ("Americana" in short. "Brand" is the name of the street where the center was located). I had heard about the place and had eaten at the Cheesecake Factory, one of a number of eateries at the Americana. Initially I ignored that neighborhood altogether, believing it would be too expensive for me. A good friend and colleague who accompanied me to my house-hunting efforts convinced me to seriously consider. I did. I bought a condominium, moved in, and have never regretted it.

Encompassing approximately nine acres and reportedly costing $400 million to build, the Americana was a mixed-use facility with multiple buildings throughout the grounds. The buildings surrounded a large central grassy area affectionately known as "The Green." The grounds were meticulously and continually maintained by a crew of groundskeepers and were always kept clean without a single piece of trash in sight. The grass was replaced every so often, according to season. The first levels of all buildings were dedicated to retail use. All the upper levels were rental properties except one building named "Excelsior," which was a condominium property sold to individual homeowners. The Americana boasted to deliver world-class retails, restaurants, and entertainment. A movie theater (Pacific Theaters Glendale 18) with stadium seating was located right on the property, and a Tesla showroom became a tenant.

Various ongoing activities took place on the Green year-round. These included concerts, dances, performances, movies under the stars in the summer, and ongoing activities for children. There was also a free trolley that ran and dinged around the perimeter of the Green every afternoon. In the middle of the Green was a two-leaf shaped water fountain that danced with music every hour on the hour from ten in the morning until nine or ten in the evening.

During the Christmas season, Santa dressed in his unmistakable red suit, walked around the property, and greeted adults and children alike. Artificial snow and choreographed, dancing fountains were displayed twice every evening throughout the holiday season. The Christmas tree was at least a hundred feet tall, one of the tallest in the country. It was truly a vibrant place. Additionally, the entire Americana community had private security with patrols day and night. Our condominium was fully secured with locked entrance accessible only with a key fob. In addition, the Excelsior also had its own twenty-four-hour security and concierge services. Never again would I be scared in this perfectly secure and immaculately clean environment—even if the doorbell were to ring in the middle of the night. I had found my perfect home; I knew that would be where I would stay. I would never need to move again.

Dancing fountain, Americana at Brand. Condominium homes in the background. There are letters engraved on the lowest tier of the gold dome: "CERCA TROVA" ("Seek and you will find," letters not discernible in this picture). My home is on the top level with arched windows decorated with green panels.

* * * * *

Years later, when I was finally emotionally ready to organize the papers Darrel had left behind, I came across one of his college assignments. The title was "Delightful Beggars," based on 2 Corinthians 8:1–7. He had handwritten a single-spaced, ten-page essay. He opened his work with this introduction:

> Even a casual reading of the passage would indicate that Paul is enjoying a genuine thrill. He is as enthusiastic as a football fan whose team has just scored a touchdown. He is ready to lay almost violent hands on any chance passer-by to tell him of the amazing and heartening experience through which he has just passed. He is sure that he has a story to tell that is infinitely too good to keep.
>
> "While in Macedonia," Paul declares joyfully, "I was literally besieged by beggars. They thronged about me with a compelling urgency. They pressed their request upon me with a determination that refused to be denied. It was indeed a most joyful experience.
>
> Now, that sounds a bit queer, does it not? As a rule, we do not like beggars. We generally seek to dodge the folks who are perpetually asking for favor. We avoid, so far as possible, those who are forever saying "where do I come in?" and "what do I get out of it?" The individual whose watchword is "gimme" is about as popular as a painful thorn. But these beggars thrilled Paul beyond all words!
>
> I wonder why?

After these powerful introductions, Darrel continued with his thoughtful arguments:

Paul found these beggars delightful because of the nature of their request. They were asking for a favor; this they confessed without shame, but the favor that they were asking is certainly refreshingly unique. Paul found it as thrilling as martial music; it was as fragrant as the perfume of violets; it was as bracing as a breeze from sun-kissed mountain. He could hardly think of their request without a shout of sheer joy.

What favor then were they asking?

What favors were they asking? He went on to present his extensive, thoughtful, and convincing arguments for why those people were "delightful beggars." To sum up: They were begging Paul for the favor of contributing to the support of the saints. "These 'beggars' had come to a new attitude toward their wealth; giving had become a joy—it had changed for them from prose to poetry, from sobs to songs. You can hear the lilt of joy in Paul's voice and catch the sparkle in his eyes across the far spaces of the centuries. It is something to thrill over!" He wrote.

Darrel got an A on his paper. The comments from his professor included these words: "It speaks to great truth … it gets the heart out of the text."

I was moved. I could feel his own character glowing through his words. It was genuine. It was true to his heart. I knew. I understood. I had witnessed him practicing what he preached: give gladly to those in need without expecting any favor in return. His life had been plagued with tragedies: losing his mother at a young age, struggling to survive with very limited resources, supporting his father and the stepmother who treated him brutally, enduring multiple surgeries and physical ailments, and confronting unrelenting leg and back pain that required strong analgesics at times, yet he never complained. His love of life never wavered, and his trust in God never faltered. He lived his life according to God's will. He practiced what he preached and what was preached to him. He should have no regrets.

My heart was filled with gratitude and contentment for having had Darrel in my life. He opened my eyes and let me see true love and humility. Overflowing with thanksgiving, I jot down the thoughts that came in my soul:

When pain and sorrow become unbearable,
Be reminded of the peace and joy he is enjoying in the presence of his Maker;
When longings to see and hold him become insufferable,
Be reassured of the day when you will meet him again in God's Kingdom.

* * * * *

Not long before his passing, Darrel introduced me to a song he had always loved. The song, "If Tomorrow Never Comes," is by one of his most favorite country music singers: Garth Brooks.

Sometimes late at night
I lie awake and watch her sleeping.

And the thought crossed my mind
If I never wake up in the morning
Would she ever doubt the way I feel about her in my heart.

So tell that someone that you love
Just what you're thinking of
If tomorrow never comes.

I listened to that song every night for weeks and months in the early days after his passing, always shedding tears with an unquenchable heartache. Tomorrow never came for him, and it would never come for me. Darrel, you have tried in every way to show me your love—the love you unconditionally committed to me will be enough to last.

I sat with a heavy yet grateful heart, full of thanksgiving for what life had gifted me.

* * * * *

"Memorials" by Emily Dickinson

> Death sets a thing significant; the eye had hurried by,
> Except a perished creature, entreat us tenderly.
>
> To ponder little workmanships, in crayon or in wool,
> With "This was the last her fingers did," industrious until.
>
> A book I have, a friend gave, whose pencil here and there,
> Had notched the place that pleased him, at rest his fingers are.
>
> Now, when I read, I read not,
> For interrupting tears, obliterate the etchings, too costly for repairs.

The interrupting tears blurred my eyes. I know Darrel is no longer here, yet I am confident that when my time comes, I will meet him again in God's kingdom.

* * * * *

Sitting in front of my computer, I look out from my sixth-floor window. The hourly display of the dancing fountain in the center of the Green begins its graceful movements in sync with the music: Louis Armstrong's "What a Wonderful World."

> I see trees of green, red roses too,
> I see them bloom, for me and you.
> -------
>
> I hear babies cry, I watch them grow.

They'll learn much more than I'll ever know.
And I think to myself: what a wonderful world.

Louis Armstrong (August 4, 1901– July 6, 1971) was one of the most influential American jazz trumpeters and singers. "What a Wonderful World" is one of my absolute favorites.

* * * * *

I snap a picture through my window. My heart is again filled with gratitude and eternal thanksgiving for being able to have a place so vibrant yet so private, so full of energy and laughter yet so quiet and personal.

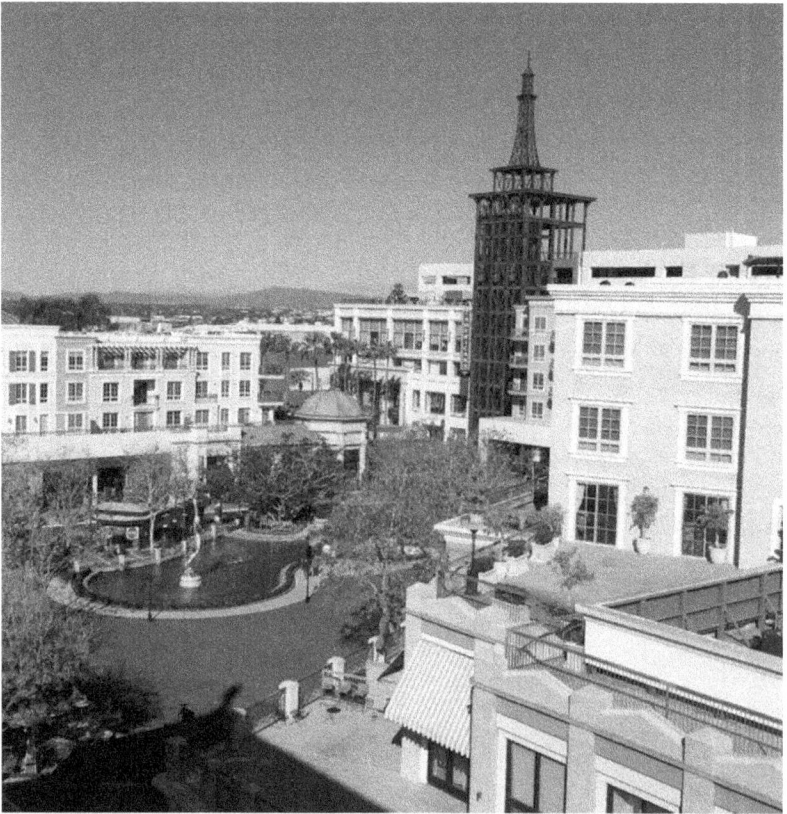

View of the Green and the retail/residential buildings from my sixth-floor window, Americana at Brand. Under a cloudless blue sky, the choreographed dancing fountain is accompanied by the music "What a Wonderful World" by Louis Armstrong.

* * * * *

Yes, what a wonderful world! And I know the sun will rise again tomorrow morning—and every morning. Even if at times, it is covered by clouds, it is there and will always be there.

I have taken the gift from God and done my best, both intellectually and practically, to give back to this wonderful world we live in. I hope I have redeemed myself for having been mercifully put on this perfectly constructed earth. I know I am blessed. While there are still unfulfilled longings and unrealized desires, I trust, as stated in another Garth Brooks song: "Some of God's greatest gifts are unanswered prayers."

www.ingramcontent.com/pod-product-compliance
Lightning Source LLC
Chambersburg PA
CBHW032006040426
42448CB00006B/505